Global Issues

General Editors: Bruce Kapferer, Professor of Anthropology,
James Cook University and John Gledhill, Professor of
Anthropology, Manchester University

This series addresses vital social, political and cultural issues
confronting human populations throughout the world. The
ultimate aim is to enhance understanding – and, it is hoped,
thereby dismantle – hegemonic structures which perpetuate
prejudice, violence, racism, religious persecution, sexual
discrimination and domination, poverty and many other social
ills.

ISSN: 1354-3644

Previously published books in the series:

Michael Herzfeld
The Social Production of Indifference: Exploring the Symbolic
Roots of Western Bureaucracy

Judith Kapferer
Being All Equal: Difference and Australian Cultural Practice

Peter Rigby
African Images: Racism and the End of Anthropology

Guinea-pigs

Food, Symbol and Conflict of Knowledge in Ecuador

Eduardo P. Archetti

Translated by
**Valentina Napolitano and
Peter Worsley**

BERG

Oxford · New York

English edition
First published in 1997 by
Berg
Editorial offices:
150 Cowley Road, Oxford OX4 1JJ, UK
70 Washington Square South, New York, NY 10012, USA

Berg is the imprint of Oxford International Publishers Ltd.

Library of Congress Cataloging-in-Publication Data

A catalogue record for this book is available from the Library of
Congress.

British Library Cataloguing-in-Publication Data

A catalogue record for this book is available from the British Library.

ISBN 1 85973 114 7 (Cloth)
      1 85973 119 8 (Paper)

Typeset by JS Typesetting, Wellingborough, Northants
Printed in the United Kingdom by WBC Book Manufacturers,
Bridgend, Mid Glamorgan.

for Peter Worsley

Contents

Preface

This book was published in Spanish five years ago. It was not exclusively written for anthropologists. One of the main aims was to introduce the Ecuadorian urban reader to the complexity of the social and symbolic worlds of guinea-pigs. For urban middle-class Ecuadorians the guinea-pig is simply an edible animal and the peasant knowledge behind it is generally unknown. My intention was to avoid some of the obscurities of anthropological jargon as well as very elaborate discussions of ethnographic findings. When I finished writing it, I felt that the result was not quite satisfactory. In many ways, the book was unnecessarily sophisticated, with too much detail for the lay reader and too little for anthropologists interested in the ethnography of the Andean region. Surprisingly, it was well received by the academic community in general, as well as by the development professionals and agencies and the general public.

The ethnographic description to be found within these pages is a contribution to the anthropology of the guinea-pig in the Andean region of Latin America. A minor topic, some will say. However, the importance of guinea-pigs as food and symbol in this part of the world is undeniable. In the great Cathedral of Cuzco, in Peru, behind the high altar, there is a painting of the Last Supper. Christ is seated with his disciples, partaking, of course, of bread and wine. But the main course in this communion meal is Indian, not Middle Eastern Judaic or Spanish Roman Catholic; the dish in the centre of the table is a cooked guinea-pig. I have not been in all the Cathedrals and churches of Ecuador but I am confident that one can find similar paintings there.

Besides ethnography, some central themes in current theoretical debates in anthropology are touched upon in this book. My interpretation of our findings shows that the impact of global institutions of modernization, state development bureaucracies and rural scientific research corporations is best understood through the observation of local cultural dynamics and sociological variations. The importance of gender, ethnicity and class when different modes of producing and appropriating knowledge are compared is made clear in the text. Globalization forces tend to destabilize the role of locality, impinging on local actors, their power relations and their applied knowledge and contribute to a dominant universality. I contest the common idea of the increasing universalization and the weakening of local knowledges and practices. My findings elucidate the co-existence in Ecuadorian society of different orders, or systems of knowledge. These differences make changes possible; one producer may be perceived as 'national' or 'global' because she adopts the new technology, while others remain local. People can thus move between different frames, being local and/or national according to their chosen practices and the origin of the resources they utilize.

The co-existence of different knowledges and practices is not without tension and conflict. The national state programme of changing 'traditional' guinea-pig production and consumption practice is part of a developmentalist ideology which has achieved an almost 'religious' status in Latin America. Developmentalism is a powerful discourse that, paradoxically enough, in spite of concrete policy implementation failures, is not abandoned or changed. The ideology of development is thus transformed into an ahistoric, rigid and encompassing frame of reference for modern planning agencies. In theory, development deals with problems that need urgent solutions and not with the 'traditional' preferences and practices of local social actors. This book shows both the limitation and the power of such an approach.

I am most grateful, above all, to the Department and Museum of Anthropology, University of Oslo, for their economic support throughout this project, especially during the process of translation. I also wish to thank John Gledhill, editor of the Global Issues Series, for welcoming with enthusiasm and intellectual generosity the project of publication suggested by Peter Worsley. Marit Melhuus, from my Department, and Kathryn Earle of Berg Publishers helped me in finding the present title. Finally, my deepest gratitude to Valentina Napolitano for working with dedication and engagement on the English translation.

Eduardo P. Archetti

Acknowledgements

This book has taken longer to write than I expected. One reason is that several researchers were involved in collecting the data. Neither the research nor the writing up of the project would have reached completion without the commitment and the intelligence of Martha Freire, Gerardo Fuentealba and Ramiro Moncayo. In the first chapter, these ups and downs are explained in more detail, and help explain the long process of maturation between my original fieldwork, back in 1983; through to a second visit in 1986; and then the editing of a preliminary report – an official publication of the Instituto Nacional de Capacitación Campesina del Ministerio de Agricultura y Ganadería of Ecuador (Ministry of Agriculture and Animal Husbandry); and, finally, this version, a short book which synthesizes a much greater body of data than is presented here. So it is an unorthodox book. The themes addressed throughout have been discussed on many occasions in my teaching activities at the University of Oslo. Yet I always had the feeling that my argument was somehow unsystematic. For these reasons, I let a lot of water run under the bridge, hoping that time would help to enrich and refine my ideas. But I still may not have been successful. Books are not like good wine.

I could have never have finished it without the generosity of my long-time place of work – the Department of Social Anthropology in the University of Oslo – which allowed me a short sabbatical in the autumn term of 1990. This gave me the opportunity of working on the preliminary text and shaping it into an acceptable length. I always thought that the subject of guinea-pigs would not be of interest to many people, and that it would, therefore, be better to reduce the original text by half. In consequence, a great deal of ethnography has been left out, but I do not regret this, because I do not believe that more detail would have helped the reader to understand either the problems or the theoretical issues any better. I have been very involved in Ecuadorean intellectual circles since 1976, and have had a close link with the Centro de Planificación y Estudios Sociales since 1978. The Centro kindly published my previous book. This renewal of trust is really remarkable. I thank especially María Cuvi, Lucía Salamea and Rafael Urriola – the present Director – for their support. Finally, here is the book we have talked about so often, with all its defects and virtues.

I recognize my personal limitations in using computers, and my resistance may make me appear incorrigibly conservative. I could certainly not have achieved anything without the invaluable help of Audun Wik, a master of electronic secrets.

Finally, I ought to thank Kristi Anne Stølen – my long-time partner – for her patience during my moody times when things did not turn out as I expected for days, sometimes for weeks, and for having encouraged me all that time. I still think that the greatest thing she has taught me is that life is not only work. I believe, however, that I have not been a good pupil. I hope I may improve.

A day in August, 1991.

CHAPTER ONE

History of a Project

This book is the result of an investigation and evaluation carried out for the Ministry of Agriculture and Animal Husbandry.[1] One part of the programme of agrarian modernization, part of the plan of Desarrollo Rural Integral (DRI) (Integrated Rural Development), was the transformation of the traditional production of guinea-pigs. Guinea-pigs had to be removed from peasant houses and kitchens. They had to abandon their reproductive and ancestral habitats, be moved away from their owners and the warmth of the household and be placed in new hutches. This logic implied that it is not possible to increase the production of the guinea-pigs without the producer obtaining maximum supervision and control over the animals' behaviour. The kitchen – the 'natural' habitat of this animal – is dark, and people believe that these animals live in a sort of reproductive chaos, where age and genetic relations are mixed randomly. Genetic engineering and the control of reproduction are central in this modern model of production. Once the guinea-pigs have left the houses, the first step in the modernization process is the achievement of improving reproductive indices. The second is to avoid genetic degeneration via careful control of breeding. The third is to place one male for any ten females in each hutch. The fourth is to avoid the rearing of very young females with characteristics that will not guarantee genetic improvement in the long run. The fifth is to sort the animals in homogeneous lots by age and by sex. The sixth is to control reproduction by removing females that are not fertile enough. The seventh is population control to maintain a low percentage of strong, sturdy reproductive samples which come from large broods. The eighth is a good handling of the newborn and to take them away from the mothers when they are twenty days old. The last point, which does not exhaust the package of possible measures, is to implement 'rational'

1

commercialization. This means eliminating those females that have given birth many times – the oldest reproductive subjects – as well as those females that have a low level of fertility and also sterile and underweight males.

Any modern model of reproduction has to take into account food as an important variable. The provision of suitable food, related to the size, sex and general conditions of the guinea-pigs, guarantees, in principle, a better transformation into food. Their diet should be based mainly on fresh vegetable matter, although the ideal diet would be a mixture of concentrated fodder.

A strong and fat guinea-pig needs to stay healthy. Therefore its health care has to be changed in order to discover quickly and precisely illnesses that afflict guinea-pigs. This implies a policy of preventive care that includes temperature control of the hutch, the elimination of humidity from the cubicles and their periodic disinfection. Once a sick animal has been discovered, it is important to treat it promptly to avoid the spread of the disease. Peasants believe that guinea-pigs are delicate animals that are continuously attacked by parasites. It is therefore necessary to disinfect them regularly.

Obviously modern handling of guinea-pigs entails controlling many variables at the same time. Genetic results depend upon food and upon health, which is itself part of a good diet. A healthy guinea-pig is, in principle, one that lives in a good habitat and has a good diet. A healthy guinea-pig grows well, puts on weight fast and reproduces quickly. In other words, the modern model of guinea-pig production calls for good planning on the part of producers, who learn to maximize the results and, therefore, behave 'rationally'. The producer has to control the context and the phases of production, to identify the distinct variables and understand their interrelations and to be aware of any variations in order to implement the necessary corrective measures. In other words, the producer (more specifically the female producer, because the rearing of guinea-pigs, as explained below, is almost entirely a female activity) needs to abandon her existing production 'code', which is determined by traditions, for a new 'set of rules' that have not yet been tried out or elaborated by others. In this way, the producer is placed in an almost experimental situation of social and cultural change, due to the fact that a change of 'code' often implies altering rules, knowledge and strategies that traditionally guide the culturally accepted productive practices.

The declared objective of the programme was to increase production and productivity, which would enable peasant families both to eat more guinea-pigs and to sell them in larger numbers. In this process, the guinea-pig would be transformed from a use value into a commodity of exchange value. Likewise, experts thought that the use of guinea-pigs would allow the active incorporation of women into the process of integrated rural development. The idea was that the transformation of a traditional system of breeding into a modern one would entail a better use of the female and domestic labour force. During this period, it was hoped that programmes of development would raise employment and income and improve diet. In this modernizing context, guinea-pigs constituted an important strategy of intervention on the part of the rural development workers and technical experts of the Ministry of Agriculture and Animal Husbandry. The guinea-pig was also a well-known, accepted and appreciated animal for the indigenous and non-indigenous peasant population in Ecuador.

None the less, the modernization programme did not progress at the pace that the planners expected. When this happens, it is common to attribute the problem to the existence of technical socio-economic 'bottlenecks' or cultural determining factors. Cultural conditioning and determining factors are normally associated with the weight of 'tradition', 'beliefs' and individual 'inertia'. These are generally the subjects of study of less quantitative social sciences, in this case social anthropology. Therefore the Ministry of Agriculture and Animal Husbandry consulted social anthropologists in order to unveil the 'cultural logic' that lay behind 'traditional' habits of livestock breeding.[2] Consequently, fieldwork was planned in an almost standard ethnographic way without any intention of testing theories and models that would have adequately explained the resistance to the new technological packets of measures. Moreover, this position was necessary because of the lack of previous work in Ecuador concerning the relation between peasant culture and the animal world – and in particular the guinea-pig.[3] Finally, an explanation of this resistance would have implied studying the existing relations between the modernization programme, and its implementation by the extension team and the subjects whose behaviour was to be changed. This went beyond the terms of reference of the study. Interestingly enough, the problem did not reside in either the technological model proposed or in the new form of animal breeding that was introduced, but in the open rejection by the women who had to carry it out.

Ecuador is a complex society, and there is no need to argue this at length. It is sufficient to mention the existence of distinct categories of female and male peasants, and their different regional, religious and ethnic traits. Since the 1960s, as a consequence of recent industrialization and increased urbanization, peasants have reproduced their cultural and productive practices in a much more complex context, in which oral tradition, coexists with written, traditional medicine, with modern medicine, and traditional technology with the world of tractors and modern inputs. Interaction between these different logics and cultural codes takes place continuously in everyday life. A clear example of this context is the active intervention of the state, through this programme of modernization and many others, in the lives of people who have kept guinea-pigs inside the house for centuries and for whom productive practice is also a way of defining domestic space. A peasant house without guinea-pigs is not, obviously, a complete house.

Social anthropology seeks to describe and explain cultural behaviours and logics by studying communities with a limited number of actors, where, by virtue of proximity and length of stay, it is possible to observe all aspects of social life together with the symbolic and ritual world. Sociologists, on the other hand, study many actors, and only a few variables. The most cited criticism of anthropological studies is their lack of 'representativeness'. In our case, we were unable to carry out traditional fieldwork, in which the guinea-pig would be located within a wider system of classification of both animal and plant worlds. We have therefore focused on the social and symbolic world of the guinea-pig. In order to minimize the consequent drawback of this focus, our approach has been twofold: carrying out the study of the guinea-pig in the greatest possible detail in an attempt to define productive and symbolic worlds, which range from economic processes through to magical beliefs, and at the same time choosing different communities on the basis of certain 'objective' criteria which, in principle, give us the opportunity to identify possible variations. The first aspect will be developed in depth in the next chapter. The second calls for a few paragraphs of explanation.

The fieldwork was carried out in eight communities. In the area of Salcedo we chose Llactahurco, Chirinche and Tigualó; in Guamote, Chismaute and Palmira Dávalos; in Gualaceo, Sharván;

and finally in Quimiag-Penipe, Ayanquil and Guzo. These communities were selected according to the following criteria: type of and control over productive resources; ethnicity; religious affiliation; and the presence or absence of a modernization programme for the breeding of guinea-pigs. Why were these criteria chosen rather than others? We thought it important that any project examining improvements in production and productivity should take into account factors which influence access to more and better pasture, but which, at the same time, increase the workload of some members of the domestic group. Consequently, we considered it a priority to delineate the location of the communities in different ecological niches, since this influences soil conditions and the possibility of increasing the production of food for guinea-pigs. At the same time, we investigated the quantity of available soil, productive strategies, the availability of pastures and grass fields, both in the mountains and in the high plateau, and the existence of irrigation, which is a fundamental factor in the production of alfalfa. All these aspects explain the importance of the first criterion. Let us analyse the remaining three.

In the world of Ecuadorean rural producers, the ethnic aspect is an important criterion for defining different systems and sociocultural logic. Generally speaking, the importance of community relations and the conservation of a busy religious and festival cycle is intimately connected to the prevalence of an indigenous peasantry at both local and regional levels. The presentation of our results will try to show – when necessary – the relevance of ethnic identity in the analysis of changes both in practices and in belief systems.

In recent years, and especially in some regions, a division between Catholic and Protestant has developed within the indigenous peasantry. We think that, if Protestant ideological discourse emphasizes aspects such as soberness, decency, cleanliness and saving, it was possible to foresee that these new values would have a precise impact on openness and receptivity to the proposed innovations. In parallel, Protestant conversion presupposes, among other things, a significant alteration of the religious and ceremonial calendar of the communities. This could imply that the guinea-pig circulates in a more restricted manner and therefore articulates fewer public, domestic and social worlds.

Lastly, we thought it was appropriate to study the impact of the projects. The degree of contact with the rural development workers varies from community to community, even within the areas where the programme of Integrated Rural Development operates. We thought, at the beginning, that the impact of the modern model of rearing guinea-pigs would had been more influential not only in the mestizo[4] communities, but also in communities that received continuous visits from the supervisors of the programmes. In order to monitor these groups we introduced the cases of Guamote and Gualaceo, where, at the beginning of our study, there were no ongoing projects focused on guinea-pigs.

The use of the multiple criteria of selection we have mentioned was based on a very simple idea, since we thought that ecological conditions and type of control over productive resources, as well as cultural and symbolic worlds associated with religion and ethnicity, influence the general understanding, beliefs and practices of the social actors. Our objective was to attempt to understand different sets of rules, the variations of the same symphony, generated by certain constraints that would, in principle, be associated with the selecting factors discussed above. Clearly, in this way, the representativeness of our study is broader and our conclusions concern a wider sociocultural field. At this level, the major problem is that of comparison, and at the same time the inclusion of all possible variations. A group of 'subcultures' of the guinea-pig exist alongside the culture of the guinea-pig around which the experts have developed their constituted 'modernization' programmes. This, therefore, introduces an additional problem: how to present our results in such a way that, acknowledging variations, the reader can still follow the flow of the analysis without getting lost in a mass of details.

An obvious alternative is to present our empirical findings community by community. However, this method entails unnecessary repetition, since the same type of practices and beliefs can be found in many different communities at the same time. The predominant trend in traditional social anthropology has been the description of integrated, homogeneous and, above all, stable cultural systems. This approximation is not only due to economy of presentation but also rests on a body of presuppositions about the way in which society and culture function, based, fundamentally, on a connection between order and social reproduction. In the first place, we shall describe what can be called the 'popular, cultural language of the guinea-pig' – the world of the guinea-pig as use value rather than exchange value (the culture of modernization). In this line of analysis we shall present communal elements that recur in every community – a sort of basic grammar. This is a description of popular practices, beliefs and concepts that constitute what may metaphorically be regarded as the 'culture of the guinea-pig'. Starting from this simple structure we shall try, subsequently, to introduce its variations. Using the distinction between restricted and extended codes, we shall move from a restricted, common and 'universal' code to an extended, individual and 'concrete' one in presenting our findings. At this level, the ethnic variable is much more relevant, more so than the religious variable, and possibly also than the economic and the ecological contexts. Therefore, variations will relate to 'mestizo' and 'indigenous culture'.

However, this type of approach remains problematic because it gives the impression that it is possible to identify clear and homogeneous cultural boundaries. In reality, and fortunately so, this is not usually the case, because social actors can always move across the boundaries of the cultures within which they operate. Social and cultural change would be unthinkable without this possibility. The existence of these boundaries – in our case the 'culture of the guinea-pig' – allows differences to be observed and, at the same time, transformation to be established as a possibility, due precisely to the existence of these discontinuities. Only the multiplicity of codes makes it possible for them to be a real choice when the moment arrives. The temporary failure of modernization programmes does not tell us anything about how the communities will react in the future. Our book is simply concerned with different sets of rules rather than 'cultural resistances'. Ideally, we would imagine our book as presenting a dialogue, an exchange of opinions between different actors about a common theme. As in daily conversation, we could continue to talk without having to agree about each topic of discussion. This open dialogue is inter-rupted only when power comes into play and only one version becomes acceptable. In the case of our present study, the obvious solution to the existence of cultural diversity is the introduction and diffusion of the culture of the experts. Paradoxically, the modernization model appears to be codified as a single alternative, as a closed system. None the less, society is an open social and symbolic space and, therefore, the history of the guinea-pig continues to develop without our being able to see how it will end.

It is central to mention that four of the communities which we have examined are typically indigenous: Llactahurco in Salcedo,

Guzo in Quimiag-Penipe and Chismaute and Palmira Dávalos in Guamote. Tigualó in Salcedo, Ayanquil in Quimiag-Penipe and Sharván in Gualaceo are mestizo communities. Chirinche and Salcedo can be considered a mixed community because the indigenous component is strong. In the matter of religion, Palmira Dávalos is the only Protestant community, the others are Catholic. It is important to point out that, at the time of our study, only six out of the eight communities which should have participated were actually taking part in the programme of modernization of guinea-pig production. In Palmira Dávalos an initial study had already taken place, but Sharván was a virgin territory.[5]

Having said this, it is important to make it clear that gender is also central. Hence, we can envisage feminine and masculine worlds within the wider context of what, until now, we have called culture in general. The guinea-pig belongs, in a clear and indisputable way, to the world of female domestic practices. The guinea-pig suggests the domestic household, the kitchen, protection against the outside – symbolic fields that refer to certain aspects of female identity. The guinea-pig – as use value – is converted into food, dishes, recipes, tastes and smells, and it is women who carry out this process of transformation. Our informants were women. None the less, we shall see later in the book that the social and symbolic world of the guinea-pig does not only involve women. The statement that the analysis of the guinea-pig refers to the analysis of the practices and belief systems of women does not imply that there is a clear-cut opposition between femininity and masculinity, the private and the public. These worlds overlap and it is possible to shift from one to the other in the same way that one crosses a national frontier without losing one's nationality. If we accept the hypothesis that a culture is built upon those borders that are crossed over, the idea of a polarization between femaleness and maleness should be combined with the idea of complementarity. In other words, the guinea-pig is a use value within Ecuadorean peasant culture for men as well as women, children and adolescents.

In the following chapter we shall present some of the general ideas that have guided our research. I am totally convinced that anthropological research depends more on our ability to generate ideas and concepts that permit us to ask the most relevant questions than on a set of techniques. To a certain extent, the attempt to understand one or more cultural logics suggests that the empirical material is reduced to 'data' through a filter constituted by our ideas and concepts. Our conclusions and findings therefore depend on our framework, the way we approach reality with our theoretical baggage and our individual sensitivity. Social actors – our informants, our 'objects' of study – speak and tell their story through our glasses and with our compasses. The problem is that, in the end, there is only one author. Hence I shall attempt to define my ideas with the great possible precision: ideas about complexity, production of meanings and cultural practices; ideas about public and private cultural worlds and the importance of explaining the sociosymbolic world of the guinea-pig from the perspective of a 'minimal' theory of rituals.

Now, we need to identify, with the greatest possible clarity, the social contexts we examined in the process of fieldwork research. The contexts are not only 'fields' for observation but also enable us to understand the data from empirically limited starting-points. In our case, the contexts will be the following: production and productive activities; food and food preparation, which indicate the process that the guinea-pig undergoes and identify who eats it, when they eat it and on what occasions; healing practices and health; and, lastly, the market that converts the guinea-pig into exchange value, the moment at which the animal is transformed into a commodity. Part of the material that is presented is an attempt at ethnographic reconstruction of ideas and practices that still exist but are not frequently practised. This body of knowledge is a kind of accumulated symbolic capital, a sort of dictionary, which, although it is not completely carried out in practice, enables us to understand the complexity of the guinea-pig as a cultural fact.

The existence of different cultural worlds leads us to discuss social and cultural change. The principal objective of this book is not an in-depth discussion of 'resistance', 'inertia' and 'tradition' in the face of modernization programmes. It is enough to say that we pose the question of transformation once we analyse different degrees of cultural complexity. At this level the hypothesis is simple – the greater the complexity, the fewer possibilities exist for rapid sociocultural change. Evidently, any process of change demands the presence of social actors to carry it out: in the case we are looking at, women were inclined to accept the new proposal. All theories of change, therefore, need not only an explicit theory of the subject – which will not be presented in this book – but also a better understanding of the positions of, and constraints upon, the

actors in a wider system in which new and old knowledge interacts
with positions of power, systems of power, roles and statuses with
hierarchical social positions. On the other hand, all changes imply
taking certain risks. Those risks cannot be understood solely at the
level of conceptual changes but must also be understood at the level
of local positions of power. The last chapter will develop this theme.
One final observation is necessary. Our findings do not follow
a quantitative model such as: 40 per cent of our informants think
x and 60 per cent think y. To make the matter more complicated,
we have to compare what is said with what is done. I do not deny
the possibility of achieving such accuracy but this was not our
purpose. We were constantly 'open' to the variability of both ideas
and practices, but with the explicit goal of recording them in
qualitative terms. This book simply attempts to connect a cultural
logic and its variations with a theoretical model of interpretation.

Notes

1. This work was carried out between September and November of 1983.
   I was responsible for coordinating the research team which was also
   composed of three young anthropologists trained in Ecuador: Martha
   Freire, Gerardo Fuentealba and Ramiro Moncayo. Later, in 1986, I
   paid a visit to Ecuador to check some of the data and to interview
   selected informants. This is a 'collective' book even if the final version
   is mine. The reader will forgive me for the fact that throughout the
   text I shall use the plural as well as the singular form in an attempt
   to demarcate distinct intellectual authorship. The plural form will
   refer less to interpretation and theoretical understanding, which is
   my own responsibility.
2. The project of evaluation and research was carried out through a
   contract between the Ministry of Agriculture and Animal Husbandry
   and the Centro de Planificación y Estudios Sociales (CEPLAES)
   (Centre for Planning and Social Studies), which has its headquarters
   in Quito. During the month of January 1984 the ministry received
   our final report of more than 400 pages. On the basis of this report,
   Dr Ruth Moya, on behalf of the ministry, and Lic. Mario Rosales,
   on behalf of CEPLAES, edited a book entitled *El Cuy en la Vida
   Campesina* (Instituto de Capacitación Campesina, Quito, 1985). This

book, although it had a print run of 2000 copies, had a limited circulation and it was fundamentally used for extension and training activities. Later I wrote an introductory and theoretical text in Norwegian (Archetti, 1986), and Martha Freire (1988) published an article in which she summed up some of the empirical findings in Palmira Dávalos and Chismaute Telán. This book can therefore be seen as the final result of our project.

3. There are three very good ethnographies about Peru: Gabriel and Gloria Escobar (1972), Bolton and Calvin (1981) and Bolton (1979). Many of the observations and findings of these ethnographers confirm the existence of an Andean cultural continuity. Thus, this book should be seen as a contribution to the 'Andean anthropology of the guinea-pig' and to a wider anthropological literature devoted to the systematic study of animals – an area of study still in formation. The works of Bolton and Calvin, even if they provide much material, still seem to me to be absorbed in a too narrow tradition: that of demonstrating that protein consumption – such as guinea-pig meat – influences the ritual cycle.

They explicitly suggest that:

the ritual cycle among Santa Bárbara people serves to share out proteins during periods in which people need them in order to stay healthy. The ritual mechanism permits the best distribution of guinea-pig meat in space and time. In fact guinea-pig meat is eaten on particular occasions which coincide with periods when dietary deficiencies are more likely, and is distributed among the whole population, flowing from those who have surpluses to those who run short of it in this period. (Bolton and Calvin, 1981, p. 391)

I think that this thesis is too extreme. In the following chapters we shall see that the guinea-pig is an ideal complement to the cycle of festivity but nothing more than that. The religious, ceremonial cycle, when guinea-pig meat is a central component of meals, cannot be explained in terms of protein deficiency, nor can ritual and symbolic practices be reduced to physiological phenomena. The spatial and temporal convergence suggests a cultural complexity that we ought to try to understand. We shall discuss these issues in greater detail in the next chapter. We shall also refer to Bolton and Calvin again in the following chapters.

4. The category of mestizo is fluid and refers to the mixing of Spaniards and American Indians.

5. This table offers a neat summary of the type of communities that we studied:

	Ecological		Farmland		Pasture		Ethnic category		Included in Integrated Rural Development guinea-pig project	
	> 3000 m	< 3000 m	Scarce	Sufficent	Scarce	Sufficent	Mestizo	Indigenous	Yes	No
Salcedo	Llacta-hurco Chirinche	Tigualó	Tigualó Chirinche	Llacta-hurco	Tigualó	Chirinche	Tigualó Chirinche	Llacta-hurco (mixed)	Tigualó Chirinche Llacta-hurco	
Quimiag-Penipa	Ayanquil Guzo	Ayanquil	Ayanquil	Guzo	Ayanquil	Guzo	Ayanquil	Guzo	Guzo	Ayanquil
Guamote	Chismaute Palmira Dávalos	Palmira Dávalos		Chismaute	Palmira Dávalos Chismaute			Chismaute Palmira Dávalos	Chismaute Palmira Dávalos	
Gualaceo		Sharván	Sharván		Sharván		Sharván			Sharván

CHAPTER TWO

The Cultural Complexity of the Guinea-pig

In many cultures people find difficulty in thinking about the role of animals. How we treat them is often inconsistent and discontinuous. Some animals live in pleasant and lavish environments, as privileged members of domestic habitats. They receive a great deal of attention and affection from their owners and are cared for by specialists when they fall ill. They become part of the household through receiving a name, which is a demonstration both of affection and individualization. The dog and the cat are particularly 'humanized' animals in the middle-class world of developed societies. However, other animals have a less pleasant life; they do not receive a name and they are reared with one primary objective – that they will become food. The care they receive does not prevent them from ending their lives in slaughterhouses or in the open field. These animals are not part of the domestic world, and their reproduction takes place outside the household, either in open fields or in special shelters away from the owner's home. These differences partly depend upon the type of animal. For instance, dogs, which are raised as pets by European, American or the Ecuadorean middle class are considered to be appetizing food in Asian cultures. Other wild animals – often ruthlessly hunted – may become objects of special treatment once they begin to live in zoos or circuses. These discontinuities indicate that in many societies one species is a focus of attention and of emotional release; others, on the contrary, are objects of consumption which therefore have to be kept at distance since they are destined to be slaughtered.[1]

The guinea-pig also falls within the twofold categorization we have suggested. In Europe and America it is a domestic animal *par excellence*, a pet for children, hence tabooed as food. In Ecuador, and generally in the Andean world, it is eaten: guinea-pigs are reared for killing. None the less, in the Ecuadorean peasant world, the guinea-pig lives inside the house together with the owners, within the same domestic space. This coexistence, or degree of intimacy, does not prevent the guinea-pig from being converted into a victim. If it were regarded as a commodity animal *par excellence*, we might think that it was just an exception. However, this is not so. It is true that the guinea-pig shares the same space with humans but it does not receive a name and, thus, maintains a sort of impersonality. To a certain extent, anonymity allows the guinea-pig to be killed and therefore to retain its condition of 'pure' animal (not 'humanized'). Moreover, guinea-pigs are not counted. They are not a population whose growth in size or diminution depends strictly upon economic or commercial criteria. Although the guinea-pig dwells in the house and is a 'domestic' animal in so far as it shares the same space with humans, its death does not provoke sorrow, as does the dramatic loss of a family's cat or dog. On the contrary, its death is an occasion for celebration and for ritual.

I have therefore decided to avoid beginning my examination of the guinea-pig's role in the cultural world of peasants by treating it as an exception where the common rule – domestic space: name: no sacrifice – is not observed. Rather, I have chosen another focus, which I consider more constructive: to introduce the cultural complexity of the guinea-pig by beginning with peasant belief systems and practices. I therefore need to consider the issue of cultural complexity.

Cultural Complexity

The concept of social complexity and its counterpart, the concept of complex societies, suggest differences of role and statuses and the specialization of area and systems of interaction. This explains why the specific roles and status that characterize particular system cannot be transferred to another one. Economic positions, for instance, cannot be automatically transposed to particular political positions. The more complex a society, the more autonomy different systems possess. The concept of cultural complexity pivots around a fundamental notion – that information circulates among different social actors – rather than the notion of a system of social positions that these actors assume. In other words, higher cultural complexity implies a higher level of information, or, rather, the production of elaborated knowledge. Although we might expect to find a strong empirical association between social and cultural complexity, this is not the case. Many oral societies studied by anthropologists are, in most cases, less socially complex than industrialized societies but do not thereby lose their cultural complexity.

The concept of cultural complexity refers to the quantity of information and knowledge produced by distinct social actors and used as a resource in dealing with key questions. Following from this, knowledge can be associated with the analysis of observable social behaviour. In parallel, it is possible to identify the context in which this knowledge actively operates. The use of this knowledge may be elaborated, even ritualized.[2] In our present study, the cultural complexity of the guinea-pig refers to the entire social context where the guinea-pig circulates and is reproduced as a medium of specific cultural practices. Since the guinea-pig is fundamentally a food, it is important to analyse the system of meals. The degree of complexity of the guinea-pig becomes deeper as we study and separate out a set of rules and practices that attribute an elaborated ceremonial content to the guinea-pig.

In this book, the semantic aspect of the analysis will be central. This enables us, therefore, to uncover the relationship between knowledge and the conditions under which such ideas are put to use. Likewise, the semantic world of the guinea-pig suggests a wider scenario in which all the animals relevant to peasant culture can be studied. The guinea-pig acquires new meanings, too, when we analyse the social context to which it belongs – when we compare it, for example, with other edible animals, such as cows, lambs and pigs, and with non-edible animals, such as dogs and cats. These oppositions allow us to understand the specificity of the guinea-pig.

Likewise, the relation between ideas, beliefs and behaviour in different social contexts – what we may call, following Bourdieu (1980, pp. 87–109), cultural practices – enables us to understand social and cultural changes. It is possible to envisage at least two situations: a decrease of information and, therefore, the specialization of the guinea-pig, for instance, as mere food; or the existence of a body of knowledge that is not articulated in concrete practices. Hence our research is based upon the assumption that complex and elaborated knowledge is related to greater use of the guinea-pig.

The guinea-pig is, in principle, a useful animal: it can be eaten and sold, and therefore belongs to the same category as many other animals. But it has little importance as an 'intermediate' product that can be transformed (e.g. as with leather, milk or wool). Nor is the guinea-pig an animal that can be used, like the horse and the ox, for other purposes, such as traction. It is not a wild animal and does not survive in the wild like other relatively small animals, such as weasels, rabbits, hares and rats. Nor it is an animal that is reared for special and distinctive religious or ritual purposes, as is the case with gamecocks. The guinea-pig is a domestic animal *par excellence*, but since it does not receive a name, as we pointed out above, it is part of a whole context of diversified practices.[3] I shall therefore attempt to describe the guinea-pig's role in the complex animal world of the Ecuadorean peasantry in greater detail rather than highlighting its specificity, and the use value of the guinea-pig will be the centre of my analysis.

Knowledge about guinea-pigs belongs to the female realm; knowledge about other animals belongs exclusively to the male sphere. Consequently this type of female knowledge is closely connected to the world of the kitchen. The guinea-pig belongs to a private world, the house, and to a closed rather than a public space. But, as we shall point out later, the use of the guinea-pig transcends the house and, at this level, female knowledge about guinea-pigs is public knowledge because it can be communicated. The social and symbolic world of the guinea-pig refers to a process in which it is possible to link together understanding, practices, positions (female status) and social identity (practices that exclude other actors).

In the first chapter I attempted to study variations of a single logic – the breeding of the guinea-pig. These are variations of 'public' culture. Obviously, a meaningful series of differences may be explained by ecological and social limitations (the cycle of domestic development) which affect only certain informants. However, it is important to relate individual variations to the local world of ideas and practices.

This short commentary on public and private worlds is relevant for the analysis of the cultural complexity of the guinea-pig. Greater complexity relates to a higher degree of behavioural structure and meaning that actors confer on it. Consequently, when we refer to complexity we refer to the existence of a world of continuity and consistency between knowledge, beliefs and behaviours. In a logical way the hypothesis of change involves both similar and different actors.

Hence, we need a model of the sociocultural world that contains discontinuities, since there will be different actors, with different types of knowledge and behaviour. In our case, it is a world that includes women, experts and rural development workers, although discontinuities of ethnicity, civil status and age are also to be found within the female world.

Furthermore, there is a strict relationship between cultural complexity and ritualization. In most modern anthropology, the analysis of ritual is no longer restricted to exclusively religious phenomena or to the world of the 'irrational'. Thus we talk about the 'celebration' of a mass, or a journey, such as a procession, as something which is ritualized, but we also conceptualize a meal or, perhaps, a football game, as a ceremony or a ritual. What do such dissimilar events have in common? Firstly, they are all social behaviours that have to follow explicit sets of rules. Secondly, they represent something that is not necessarily reducible to some merely instrumental content. Social actors have different degrees of participation and comply with sets of rules and symbols which influence their involvement and which they have to observe. Thirdly, and finally, their actions have a special significance which it is possible to observe. In my analysis, when I refer to the symbolic world of the guinea-pig, I refer to the relation between multivocality and ritualization (Tambiah, 1981).

Any public situation in which different types of knowledge and practices confront each other calls for the analysis of power.[4] Power has both a material base of reproduction and an ideological component. In my opinion any ritual action is a manifestation of power. Ritual is not mere illusion, but a very effective means of exerting and seeking power. The dramatic content of rituals cannot be understood without this dimension of power, which establishes conditions of liminality.[5]

The model of cultural complexity, therefore, needs to clearly distinguish those social contexts in which guinea-pigs are used (production and circulation) from those in which they are not (consumption and selling). These contexts, and their borders, have to be understood as methodological tools for analysing the guinea-pig and the different realms to which it belongs. In the next section I shall present those contexts, in the simplest and most concise way possible.

Producing the Meat: Production and Productive Practices

It should now be clear that the producers of guinea-pigs are also its main consumers. It is production or, better, domestic breeding that intimately connects the guinea-pig to the development of the domestic cycle. Following this line of enquiry, we can distinguish two different phases in the productive process. Firstly, our observations are orientated to an understanding of the domestic world of the guinea-pig: the importance of the household, the warmth and smoke of the peasant kitchen. We need to find out how their habitat is related to beliefs about temperature and the importance of smoke and of leftovers used as food. In the following pages, we shall see how smoke both affects the inner quality of the guinea-pig – the taste of the meat – and is an external protection against certain types of illnesses. Secondly, we focus on genetic, reproductive handling, where reproductive practices and the beliefs attached to them are central. The next step is to develop a taxonomic model for different types of guinea-pigs, a model that is fundamental for understanding their reproductive logic.

First let us look at the classification of plants and herbage. In order to begin our understanding of the guinea-pig's diet, we used two criteria: edible/non-edible and, within the edible, the best and the worst food. We found that it was important to analyse criteria of food quality and to try to discover the logic of preferences in terms of which producers correlate 'efficacy' with other standards, such as good taste, the quantity of fat and the texture of the meat. Following this line of thought, and taking into account also the logic of cold/hot, which is dominant in the Ecuadorean symbolic world, we tried to investigate the deep relations between the various elements of diet.

Indisputably, there is no animal productive practice in which practices of health and hygiene are absent. Hence, herbage and plants are used as food as well as remedies. Any system of 'traditional' diet implies a classification of illnesses, their causes and the best way of getting rid of them. Consequently, we need to ask whether the guinea-pig has a relevant therapeutic role in the healing of other animals.

At the level of the productive process itself, we consider it important to distinguish responsibilities within the domestic group: who is in charge of the rearing; who, eventually, collect plants and herbage and how this is done. At the same time, we examine the relationship between the rearing of guinea-pigs and broader productive strategies, in order to measure the degree of autonomy in relation to the marketing of inputs and the selling of products. Maximizing the quantity – planning the quantity of food in relation to the numbers and the types of guinea-pigs – implies the introduction of general market mechanisms into the productive schema. We therefore need to explore the way in which the logic of domestic production involves market relations or does not.

The Meat Transformed: Eating and Cooking the Guinea-pig

The guinea-pig has a central role in traditional Ecuadorean cooking. One of the aims of our research was to follow the transformation of the guinea-pig into 'food'. Therefore, we have to ask what 'food' is. 'Food' is more than a set of products and raw ingredients with a certain nutritive value which permit the members of a domestic group to reproduce. It is also a set of rules of behaviour and a system of communication, a body of images and flavours that refers to a system of usage linked to social contexts and social occasions.[6] Consequently, a dietary model is a specific way of classifying, valuing and establishing hierarchies in the world. This is done by choosing some foods, out of a wide range, in accordance with taboos, and, secondly, by transforming them arbitrarily via recipes and techniques of cooking (grilling, frying, boiling, baking, smoking, curing). In the symbolic world of the guinea-pig, a variety of recipes are used.

Guinea-pig can be eaten in different ways. Therefore, we need to look into the guiding principles. The ideal, unstructured diet is the snack. Here, there are no fixed rules about ways and times of eating, and no drinks to go with the food. A snack, like a snack bar, is very informal, with no specific or fixed mealtimes and no strict ceremonial. Structured consumption, on the contrary, implies an elaborated code that establishes the place, the time and the sequence of consumption. Therefore, the idea of a 'real' meal implies highly structured consumption. The most 'ideal' meal, in the end, is a 'banquet', where service, dress, seating-places and the exchanging of toasts take place in accordance with a set of fixed and explicit rules, which are very difficult to flout. A banquet is also a temporal sequence, which is often multifaceted and where there is no time pressure or informality. The snack – as with a hamburger or hot dog – is a symbol of an industrial society, where there is 'no time' and whose social relations are intermittent. It is probably because of this that hamburgers and hot dogs (a meat that does not present resistance, surrounded by disposable items – napkins, or mustard sachets, salt and pepper and cleaning tissues) are symbols of time pressure in modern society. The banquet, on the contrary, is a system of resistances: its length appears endless and etiquette has to be maintained.

Moreover, it is possible to consider meals as forming a cycle, ranging from everyday meals to special meals. An ordinary meal is not connected with social situations related to specific ceremonial cycles, to rites of passage such as first communion, wedding, death or other religious ceremonies. In this context, Sunday or any other special day calls for special meals: exceptional conditions that involve a system of status and prestige, in which the combination of structured and exceptional consumption is opposed to ordinary, everyday unstructured consumption, as well as to everyday struc-tured consumption. Almost by definition, the combination of special and unstructured consumption does not exist.[7]

The logic of these combinations suggests that the consumption of structured/exceptional meals is rarely transformed into daily/structured consumption. This would be the case, for instance, if the European middle class ate turkey every day rather than only at Christmas. Turkey can be eaten every day, e.g. as a 'sandwich' – a sort of snack – without the decorations, the condiments and the vegetables used at Christmas. Structured/exceptional consumption is thus a cluster of events and situations with a strong ritual con-notation. This kind of consumption is at the top of the culinary system.

The world of meals is not exhausted by this typology, because we have also to situate them within a social context. The typology allows us to classify events, but does not tell us anything either about the actors or the place where the eating takes place. In this respect, snacks, as well as banquets, can be both public and private.

In the case of the guinea-pig, we therefore need, to look at the domestic context in which members of the family eat it. Since there is a hierarchical system, we need to look at the status of the consumers (men, women, children, the old and sick people) and then when, how and which part of the guinea-pig is eaten. The first implication of this analysis is that we have to identify the kind of domestic space which may or may not be present as hierarchical or differentiated. This involves a fundamental and complex dynamic between the system of representations involved in the context of consumption and the social characteristics of the consumers. When we mentioned consumers, we included sick people. Regardless of age and sex, ideas about health and sickness influence the position of a food in a system of meals. The guinea-pig is no exception to the general rule that food is related to wider ideas about sickness. Unhealthy food can cause sickness and therefore belongs to the bodily functions which are most carefully thought about, in many cultures.

The life of a whole family is subject to a cycle of domestic development and at each stage expansion, fission and fusion are marked by culinary rituals. We therefore examine how different rites of passage – weddings, births, baptisms, first communions and death – involve the consumption of guinea-pigs.

But peasant social relations cannot be reduced to the domestic sphere. The reproduction of their system of social relations includes horizontal relations, such as kinship, godparenthood and friendship, as well as vertical relations, such as those with landowners, priests, politicians, bureaucrats, doctors, lawyers and businessmen. It is at this point that guinea-pig is turned into food; becomes an 'offering', a 'thanksgiving' or a 'payment'. At the same time, it becomes an effective social instrument for categorizing situations and for reproducing and defining changes in systems of social relations.

We need, then, to distinguish the cultural logic of the guinea-pig in private and public contexts, in kinship ties and in wider social relations. Obviously, the public realm – at both local and regional levels – is associated with a complex calendar of religious feasts. There is no religious celebration without noise, glitter, dance, music, drinking to excess and, obviously, food. Ecuadorean religious feasts require a great deal of consumption of guinea-pigs. This consumption especially falls on those who hold religious offices in the community. We have tried to follow the 'exchange' and 'circulation' of guinea-pigs on these occasions, paying particular attention to the place of the *priostes*[8] in them. Our data show that some *priostes* can use up to fifty guinea-pigs on particular ceremonial occasions. Likewise, when a family goes on a pilgrimage, with the aim of fulfilling a promise or of calling on the Virgin or on saints, it is common to make an 'offering' of guinea-pigs. The calendar of celebrations cannot be restricted to the religious calendar, though, because there are a whole set of social and political events which punctuate individual and community life. Guinea-pigs are eaten when there is a municipal feast; at the inauguration of a school, a bridge or a new road; or when people celebrate the installation of water-pipes. Communal gatherings for voluntary labour usually end up with the consumption of guinea-pigs and plenty of alcohol.

When the guinea-pig becomes food, it is 'destroyed' – consumed – as flesh, and therefore disappears. The different contexts in which this takes place show that the producers have to have a strategy of production that recognizes this. A Protestant community, for instance, does not need to produce the same quantity of guinea-pigs as a Catholic community, because it celebrates fewer ceremonies. Therefore, we shall need to look at the consumption of guinea-pigs as representing a much wider social and symbolic world than that defined by the mere satisfaction of the need for protein.

The guinea-pig belongs to the domestic and female world. Its transformation into food depends on women and their culinary skills. So there is no woman without her guinea-pigs. But the opposite is possible: there are men with no guinea-pigs. In other words, the death of a wife also implies the death of her guinea-pigs, except when a daughter is available to take over their breeding. The guinea-pig is a much more gendered animal than other Ecuadorean animals, domestic or wild.

The Guinea-pig as Benefactor: Health and Curing Practices

We mentioned above that in any society health and illness play a central role in belief systems and cultural practices. Ecuadorean peasant cultures are no exception. We shall not attempt to describe the complex system of classification of illness in Ecuadorean peasant society. My concern is simply to see what the role of the guinea-pig is in the Ecuadorean rural world.[9] The use of herbage and medicinal plants is a major part of its therapeutic practice, and a special diet is often suggested. Both weeds and plants and special diets will thus have special therapeutic properties. It is important, therefore, to investigate the intrinsic properties of the guinea-pig and how those properties are transmitted when guinea-pigs are eaten.

In Ecuador, food and diet are seen as linked to particular kinds of illnesses and are analysed on the basis of two principles: the opposition between hot and cold, and, at the same time, the search for an equilibrium between these forces and the principles underlying them.[10] Ideas of equilibrium are seen as related to the inner working of the body as well as to the temperature of the environment. These ideas act as powerful ways of classifying plants, herbage, vegetables and animals. In parallel, they work as a system of general orientations that inform action and a whole set of cultural practices. These principles can be seen, for example, in productive strategies, such as taboos, in the elaborate and rich Ecuadorean cuisine, in combining maize and fertilizers, or in practices and rituals related to traditional health care. The existence of these principles and their multivocality are manifestations of the cultural complexity to which I have referred earlier.

Let us return briefly to the matter of therapies. Therapies are effective for a sick person only if they have both an instrumental and a symbolic efficacy. This involves two things: on the one hand, the actors have to believe in the efficacy of particular ritual 'signals' (señales), signs that are intimately associated with the management of the situation by the 'experts'. On the other hand, patients develop a special sensitivity towards particular symbols that condense and summarize meanings at different levels. The use of the guinea-pig as symbolic articulator and revealer of secrets in the healing massages (sobada) has both these qualities. It was not our intention to describe traditional health care in rural Ecuador,[11] but only to record the presence of the guinea-pig in the healing massage. We did not study massage healers. We were interested in seeing how informants conceptualized the healing massage as a diagnostic mechanism and as part of the curative process. Consequently, we focused on the second stage of the ritual, in which the guinea-pig 'sucks out the disease', although this leaves the healer out of the analysis, and thereby, without doubt, loses insights into a central character in this ritual. In this therapeutic practice, the guinea-pig is conceived as an 'instrument' that absorbs and retains the disease, 'codifies' it and transmits it back to the healer. The healer interprets and deciphers something that is in the animal's body. Thus, the use of the guinea-pig makes possible more accurate diagnosis. This property is instrumental and intrinsic to the guinea-pig – in other words, its privilege.

The last aspect of our analysis relates to the use of the guinea-pig in the treatment of certain diseases of large animals. We thought we would find the guinea-pig being used in the treatment of other smaller animals, because it has specific therapeutic properties and is of great efficacy. Since peasants value their animals, and veterinary surgeons are far away, they rely on own local veterinary knowledge.

The Guinea-pig as a Commodity: a Market Analysis

In commercial economies, the market is the final destiny of products – the place where a set of use values is converted into exchange value. The sale of the guinea-pig is thus a sort of final transformation – its metamorphosis into an object that acquires a price.

Ecuadorean peasants produce both use value and exchange values. In this type of economic context, it is especially interesting to examine the way in which products circulate in the market, or, to be more precise, the degree of commoditization of different plants, fruits and animals. So we examined the way in which, in the domestic sphere, guinea-pigs relate to other animals and products that enter the market. We might have argued, without further discussion, that the guinea-pig is at the margin of the logic of commoditization, because it is imbued with special meaning. However, we also tried to see if there is a set of restrictions on commoditization, which arise from the domestic cycle, from pressure on female labour and from the market itself (e.g. unattractive prices, the absence of access to the market, lack of demand). Obviously, an increase in production and maintenance of a commercial logic imply a stable relationship with the market. Market stability depends on a steady, and preferably increasing, demand. From the producers' perspective, urban centres are therefore the most important. The expansion of trade also depends upon the way in which the guinea-pig is consumed in the villages and towns of the sierra. If consumption is highly structured and exceptional – as we argued above – we would expect restricted problems of supply to occur at peak times for celebrations. Therefore, only an increase in daily consumption could bring about a rapid increase in commercial transactions. In this process, only industrialized slaughter and refrigeration could guarantee stable demand, especially if guinea-pig meat was being consumed by the urban population. On the other hand, in situations in which the guinea-pig's use value predominates, we should expect more unpredictable market behaviour from producers: that is, that guinea-pigs are sold only when there is a shortage of cash and that, by the same token, they are very rarely purchased.

The transformation of the guinea-pig into a special food in traditional and mestizo restaurants is one important aspect. The killing of guinea-pigs and their transformation into a commodity acquire a special meaning in this context, since it is not only the way they are prepared which is important but also the days on which they are consumed and their price.

By Way of Conclusion

The analysis of the guinea-pig in these different contexts allows us to see how belief systems acquire meanings through cultural practices and are tied to a set of social relations, in arenas in which different degrees of ritualization are associated with the life and death of the animal. My analysis should therefore be linked to the more general problem of forms of local knowledge in a situation of social and cultural change in which the state intervenes with new discourses of and plans for development. Our actors and their communities are immersed, in fact, in a social world characterized by urban migration and continuous expansion of modern services: health centres, schools, development agencies and new commercial networks. The world of the guinea-pig can therefore only be another point of intervention and penetration of alternatives. The model of analysis that I have presented, in which cultural complexity is the Gordian knot, does not exclude either change or continuity. Culture and the socio-economic worlds of our actors are changing rather than static elements. Even resistance to the technological innovation advocated by technicians and experts, who represent 'modernity', is in itself a dynamic phenomenon. We cannot simply say that women are 'traditionalists': they are challenged by new dilemmas and possibilities and are forced to make choices. I shall discuss this issue further in the final chapter of the book.

Notes

1. See Serpell (1986) and Digard (1990) on this twofold animal condition. A general discussion of this theme can be found in Ingold (1988). We should not forget that the constitutive element in the domestication of animals is clearly their consumption. In consequence, it may be important to maintain the distinction between domestic and domesticated animals. Consumption shapes productive systems associated with animal breeding, and thereby the ways in which they are herded and protected, their feeding and reproduction. The degree of technical development, and therefore the particular methods used, and the wider ecological conditions are elements that make it impossible to 'predict' the likely outcome of production in particular situations. This does not, however, reduce the importance of examining animals within a context of social relations with humans, in which strategies of use and consumption are central. To eat or not to eat a domestic animal is a complex and often subtle choice. Animals play political, symbolic and emotional roles, which vary from society to society. A detailed examination of animal classification is therefore called for. Following this line of thought, Borneman (1988) has shown that ideas used in breeding and classifying horses in North American society first appeared in the categorization of human beings. Hence, the world of animal species is influenced by a wider social world, in which social practices and the construction of national identities play a preponderant role.
2. My analysis of cultural complexity is based on the approach of Douglas and Gross (1981).
3. Digard's analysis (1990) is undoubtedly the best introduction to anthropological analysis of domestic animals.
4. For a more detailed discussion of the relationship between ritual, power and social integration see Lukes (1977, pp. 30–51).
5. See Turner (1974, pp. 23–55 and 98–115). This association is missing in the work of Turner. However, we can read between the lines in

his work that the symbolic efficacy of different rituals is influenced by their dramatic power, which rests on the polarization of meanings.

6. The best introductory anthropological analysis of food and cooking is still Goody's book (1982). As a historical introduction, Tannahill (1973) is also a useful work. However, my personal preference inclines towards three articles – one written by Douglas (1975, pp. 249–75), the second by Barthes (1979) and the third and last by Fischler (1980).

7. Nicod (1975) has discussed four categories in analysing the eating habits of the British: the occasional meal, the structured event, the snack and the meal. An occasional meal takes place when people eat without having a proper meal. A structured event takes place when it is possible to observe rules that dictate the time, the place and the particular sequence which forms a 'special' type of meal. The 'snack' is an unstructured event. Lastly, the 'meal' in a strict sense is strongly regulated and it is impossible to alter sequences and combinations. Douglas adds the categories of different 'special' and 'ordinary' events to these classifications. Whether food consumption is either structured or unstructured, or everyday or exceptional, clearly defines these different types of meal. Our typology accepts these distinctions but at the same time retains the advantage of simplicity. The empirical findings in the excellent issue of *Ecuador Debate* (1985) about food in Ecuador can be subsumed by my typology. In the different articles peasant food systems are distinguished by various degrees of structure and types of event. The empirical data show that guinea-pigs are reared in almost every domestic group and are never an unstructured, everyday food.

8. An office in a brotherhood, a confraternity or a kinship-related group. The *priostes* often play culturally important roles in religious rituals [translator's note].

9. See Sánchez Parga *et al.* (1982) for a discussion of the relationship between health and peasant society in Ecuador.

10. Gerardo Fuentealba writes:

The organism, as an expression of nature, is not detached from ideas about nature. It is a multifaceted unity composed of elements classified through the binary principle of hot and cold. For instance, the head may be considered hot and the feet cold so that their interaction produces a situation of vital bodily equilibrium; the maintenance of this equilibrium promotes health: its disruption leads to sickness. Consequently, diet – an activity which maintains the reproduction of the body – should be orientated towards preserving this equilibrium in the same way as clothes and shelter, which also protect the body from outside agents. Where this equilibrium is disrupted diet plays a vital part in restoring it through 'preventive' practices in some cases and illnesses in others. Therefore, norms and rules guide the selection, combination and preparation of food, and are used to reach the above-mentioned balance and equilibrium. (Fuentealba, 1985, p. 185)

Obviously this conception is not peculiar to Ecuadorean culture, because the majority of the great 'civilizations', as well as many societies with oral, preliterate traditions, have shared the belief – or still do share it today – that it is important to maintain bodily equilibrium, and therefore to avoid excessive bodily heat or coldness. McKee (1988) rightly points out that in Ecuador there is an interplay between the Spanish idea of 'cold' and 'hot', which derives from a classification of humour and of Indian ideas about these categories, neither of which relates only to hot and cold temperature. Thus, some foods heat up the human physiological system while others cool it down – something that depends more on the food's effects on the organism than on its intrinsic temperature. I shall come back to this point when I discuss the therapeutic properties of the guinea-pig.

11. Barahona's ethnographic description of healing massage using guinea-pigs (Barahona, 1982) is still valid. However, his analysis of the massage healer and his/her practices, the patients, the complex ritual settings and the process of diagnosis is not focused around the use of the guinea-pig, since he does not ask why people use guinea-pigs and not other animals or, even more importantly, why the guinea-pig is a technical instrument in ritual, matters which, in my opinion, are crucial to understanding the guinea-pig as a symbolic focus.

CHAPTER THREE

The Meat Produced

In this chapter I shall focus on a few central aspects of the production of the guinea-pig as edible 'meat'. Thus, the guinea-pig
appears to be a 'product' that requires special attention when it is
killed. Obviously the meat is not the whole of the animal, since
the entrails of the guinea-pig are eaten, but not the brain or the
skin. Nevertheless, because the guinea-pig is a small animal,
weighing between 600 and 1000 grams when slaughtered, almost
the entire body is meat, and so it is roasted as a single piece. It is
impossible to hide the form of the traditional animal presentation
of grilled guinea-pig, except when it is chopped into pieces and
cooked in soups or stewed. The physical appearance of the guinea-
pig reminds people of non-edible animals that have a similar bodily
constitution, such as weasels and rats. So, for people who belong
to other cultures, eating guinea-pig often seems a horrific and
repugnant act, because consuming its meat seems similar to eating
rats or a beloved children's pet.

The 'meat' is therefore a social product, a body that is consumed
like any other cultural object regarded as edible.[1] Hence, it is
necessary to rear guinea-pigs, giving them a habitat that is suitable
for their reproduction; to provide a proper and regular diet; and
to prevent illnesses. The guinea-pig needs the same care as that
provided for any domestic animal that is to be slaughtered. In the
next few pages we shall try to portray briefly the process through
which the guinea-pig is turned into meat. Before that, though, we
shall give a brief introduction to the animal itself.

Characteristics of the Guinea-pig

The guinea-pig – *cuy* in Latin American Spanish and *quwe* in Quechua – like the llama and the alpaca, is an edible animal that is native to the Andean region, domesticated before the Spanish conquest. The guinea-pig belongs to the family of Caviidae, which is genetically closer – despite its appearance – to the chinchilla or the porcupine than to the mouse or the rat.[2] Archaeological data suggest that the guinea-pig was domesticated around AD 1000. We may imagine that the guinea-pig was not only part of the diet but, from the beginning, became another occupant of the native dwellings. Therefore, their original captivity – within dark shelters – contributed to their rapid domestication. The result of this technique can be seen in the fact that the guinea-pig is undoubtedly a dusk and night animal. It tries to avoid both strong light and total darkness. Its physiological activities continue throughout the night, since it does not fall into complete relaxation or into sleep, as other animals do. Moreover, it is a 'wet' animal, able to expel up to a tenth of its total body weight with its urine.

On the other hand, both dietary and 'social' qualities must have played a predominant role in the process of genetic selection in the past. Nowadays Indians' guinea-pigs are particularly noisy creatures, both because of their constant screams and grunts, and because they constantly call out to gain their owner's attention. In the past, the Indians tried to select for the noisier animals in preference to the quieter ones. This, however, is not to deny the general impression that the guinea-pig is a 'shy' animal, especially in front of people it does not know. One informant characterized the guinea-pig as a 'shy and nervous' animal, two characteristics that do indeed typify its behaviour.

During the Inca empire, the guinea-pig was important both in people's diet and in the ceremonial world. Llamas and alpacas belonged to the state, whereas the guinea-pig was the 'popular' animal *par excellence*. There is clear evidence that guinea-pigs were consumed only on ritual occasions and were never part of the everyday peasant diet. Various chronicles emphasize that the guinea-pig was slaughtered and eaten only on festive occasions or when making offerings to the gods.[3] At the same time, the guinea-pig was used as an instrument in divination. There is no evidence that it was used as a totem.

Guinea-pigs were more widely distributed before the Conquest,

and were found over a great part of what is now Chile and northern
Argentina. Today the breeding and use of the guinea-pig are concentrated among peasants living in the areas of the central Andes:
in Bolivia, Peru and Ecuador and part of southern Colombia (in
the region of Nariño). However, its consumption has spread outside rural areas, and it is now found as a 'typical' food in various
large and middle-sized towns in these countries. But guinea-pig is
still a peasant food *par excellence*.

At first sight, it is difficult to distinguish the male from the
female. The only criterion used is head size, since the male may
have a slightly bigger head. Among the most common kinds in
Ecuador, the adult guinea-pig can grow to as much as 25 centimetres in length and 1000 grams in weight, the average being 22
centimetres and 850 grams. Guinea-pigs begin to eat regularly
when they are four months old and weigh 500 grams. Female
puberty occurs at around 60 and 70 days, and for the male puberty
is at about 80 days. The period of gestation varies from litter to
litter. It is longer when there is only one offspring (nearly 70 days)
and shorter with multiple litters (between 66 and 68 days). According to our informants, birth takes place during the night, and the
mother takes care of disposing of the placenta, which is then licked
and eaten. As one of our informants said: 'In the morning, the
mother appears with its cleaned and healthy offspring, having
given birth in the darkness of the night, which they consider to be
favourable. When they give birth during the day, it is as if they were
asking for help.' A few minutes after birth, the babies start to walk
and suck milk. At this point, they do not create any particular
problem. Guinea-pigs can live for up to eight years and are fertile
– in theory – until that age. However, according to our informants,
female fertility decreases from the fourth year onwards.

If one wanted to defend the guinea-pig as a 'multifaceted and
functional' animal, one could say that it is strong, is not demanding,
is tame, eats, in principle, anything and is docile and easy to handle
if not exposed to changes in temperature. Moreover, it is an
efficient and cheap source of protein: its meat provides 20.5% of
protein against the 14.5% for pork, 16.4% for mutton and 17.5%
for beef. In a world where a slim figure is important, guinea-pig
meat has little fat: only 7% against 40% for pork and 31% for lamb.
Obviously in Ecuadorean peasant culture the guinea-pig is not only
nutritious, but is also the 'hottest' meat.

The Habitat of the Guinea-pig

Knowledge about guinea-pigs and ways of rearing them belongs –
as mentioned above – to the feminine realm. The guinea-pig
'belongs' to the house; its habitat is the kitchen, in proximity to
the fireplace. The domestication of the guinea-pig has resulted in
a view of these animals as 'weak' and in need of careful protection
if their survival is to be guaranteed. It is commonly believed that
a guinea-pig living in the wild would only survive a few hours
because it would be attacked by other animals or would simply not
know how to survive, what food to eat and where to find it. The
rabbit, on the other hand, because of its kinship with the hare, is
seen as a small animal that is better equipped to survive in the wild.
People think that rabbits can at least run fast, while the guinea-
pig cannot even do this, since it moves slowly and wearily, stopping
all the time, and is also easily frightened.

This is why the guinea-pig lives in the kitchen or in shelters next
to the house that communicate with it. This second arrangement
allows them to sleep in the kitchen at night. However, in some
cases, women prefer to keep them in the kitchen even during the
day, and allow them to sleep near the fireplace. When they are in
the kitchen, women often make a special corner for them, close
to the fire. This area is separated off by a barrier of cement or mud;
in other cases, the guinea-pigs wander freely through the house
(since peasant houses consist of only one room divided up according to 'function').

Guinea-pigs that live in the kitchen cannot be attacked by their
enemies. Cats and dogs belong to the category of their enemies,
and are therefore not kept inside the house. In order to prevent
dogs developing a taste for guinea-pigs, they are systematically
prevented from entering the house and are also forbidden to eat
the guts of the guinea-pigs when they are slaughtered. So people
usually bury the entrails or take particular care to give them to the
pigs. Cats are particularly likely to harm guinea-pigs, because they
are 'vicious' and peculiarly malicious.

None the less, the main enemy of the guinea-pig is the *chuchuri*,
a sort of wild weasel, which has an amazing ability to sneak into
shacks and an innate 'mad' craving for guinea-pigs. In Indian
communities, people considered this animal – which is called
llangarico – very bloodthirsty: its main interest is in killing guinea-
pigs in order to drink their blood and eat their eyes and ears. To

stop them entering the guinea-pig shelters, when *chuchuri* are around people boil dry fish with coriander, thinking that the smell keeps them at bay, or spread ashes outside the house in the belief that this will prevent them from coming in. When people think that a *chuchuri* has got into the house, they try to evict it by making a loud noise, especially with metallic objects, and, at the same time, roasting the strongest kind of chili on the fire. Wild rats or *pericotes* belong to this same 'beastly' category, although their predilection is only for young guinea-pigs. This animal is also considered to be 'inauspicious', because it can announce the approaching death of a loved and close relative.

Toads can be indirectly damaging. Ecuadorean peasants believe that toads, and especially their urine, are very harmful to guinea-pigs. Therefore people take a lot of care to see that there are no toads in areas where they collect plants. They believe that there are four dangerous types of toads, which can be distinguished by their colour and size; a black one, called *hambatu*; one that is greeny-white in colour, which is normally called a 'toad'; the *kaila*, wholly green; and finally the *chukcki*, which is smaller and is coffee-coloured. It is believed that, when toads urinate on plants, they transmit diseases of the intestine, which lead to swelling of the stomach and, eventually, the death of the guinea-pig.[4]

The guinea-pig needs to be protected not only from its enemies but also from the cold. In a very general way, I can say that the strongest belief we found was that of maintaining a stable temperature. The ideal place for guinea-pigs to live is in the house and consequently around the kitchen fireplace. People make great efforts to keep their houses at a moderate temperature, neither very hot nor very cold. When, for instance, they cook for a long time, they take care to open the door from time to time, more to avoid excessive heat than to let the smoke or steam out. Likewise they take care to close doors when there are strong winds. These beliefs function as a great constraint when the moment arrives for people to think about letting guinea-pigs out of the house. The nature of the sierra, with its sudden changes of temperature, its cold winds, freezing dusk and harsh nights, introduces factors which, from the producers' standpoint, are impossible to control. The fireplace, on the other hand, provides the right temperature for the rearing of guinea-pigs. Even if people use gas or paraffin stoves to prepare breakfast quickly, they still use the traditional fire to cook lunch and afternoon meals.

Another important factor that defines the ideal habitat of the guinea-pig is the idea that the smoke of the kitchen wards off a whole set of harmful parasites that can cause certain types of diseases (see below). Related to this is a strongly rooted belief that smoke influences the taste of the meat: a guinea-pig that has been raised in the kitchen has a different taste from those which have been reared outdoors. Even informants who had never had the opportunity to compare the taste of different animals themselves still argued that this was so or that somebody who knew a lot about it had told them so. In our interviews, the association between smoke and taste was clear, because guinea-pig meat is rather sweet. People think that the smoky taste produces a very appetizing combination which improves the taste of the meat and makes it less 'bland', 'less sweet'.[5]

The guinea-pig, moreover, functions as an efficient 'waste-disposer' in the kitchen, because it eats scraps thrown away during the preparation of meals. Guinea-pigs eat any sort of peel – onion, carrots and beans – maize leaves and 'rotten' maize which is unsuitable for cooking, as well as all kinds of grain and leftovers. People do not agree about potato peelings: in some communities, people believe that potato peelings are a good food; in other communities they do not, because they are thought to cause diarrhoea. I shall come back to this point when I review the way people use a nutritional model.

Reproduction and the Genetic Model

The birth of each litter coincides with the beginning of a recently married couple's life and with the couple's settling into a new house. The woman moves with the guinea-pigs which she has started to breed and which she received from both her parents (especially her mother) and her godparents after her wedding. Generally the original litter includes a *yayacuy*, which has more fingers than usual, and between two and ten females. Later on, all the male progeny of the *yayacuy* will receive the same nickname. The criteria of selection of the animals vary, but they include size and weight (the best are the fattest and healthiest), as well as quietness and 'good character'. People think that the *yayacuy* is more powerful and transmits these qualities to its male and female progeny. The *yayacuy* remains fertile for up to three years. The female does not show any visible sign that it is fertile. No particular colours are preferred; that is a matter of individual aesthetic taste. As far as the length of the fur is concerned, people prefer animals with short coats, one reason being that the fires in the kitchen are very close to the ground and, since guinea-pigs that have a lot of hair tend to shed it, it can get into cooking pans.

When breeding, there is no separation by age or sex; guinea-pigs 'mix together at random'. In the words of one of our informants, 'they mate with us not knowing which is Dad and which is Mum'. However, this is not really true, because there is control over reproduction. The usual technique is not to allow several adult males in a litter to survive. This is done in several ways. The first is by castrating males older than three years old. The second is by eating males which have attained a certain weight – 500 or 600 grams – and which are about to begin their reproductive stage. Our informants generally agreed that it is better to have only a few active males in each litter, since otherwise this is an invitation to conflict and fights in the group. Fights occur not only between males but also when females are 'full' and consequently resist mating again. The strategy, therefore, is to keep one or two active *yayacuyes* to maintain a sort of harmony in the litter, in the kitchen and in the house. Normally people think that one male can easily mate with fifteen females.

In Indian communities, the standard classification includes – together with the *yayacuy* – the *güagüacuy*, which are young animals, up to two months old, of either sex. Then, there are the *maltones*, which are already in the reproductive stage, but which have not reproduced.[6] Among these we can distinguish males, which are called *cari*, and females – *huarmi*. When females have given birth for the first time, or are going to, they are often called *maduras* ('mature'). Hence maturity is achieved at six months of age. The difference between male *maltones* and *maduros* has consequences for their fate as meat: *maltones* are normally cooked, while *maduros* are roasted. The reason for this is simple: the meat of the *maltones*, being young animals, is blander and less fatty than the meat of the *maduros*, which are normally bigger and older.

In Indian communities, the system of classification is more complicated, but less connected with reproduction. It entails skin colour: *muru*, where the guinea-pig has more than two colours; *pinto*, when it has two colours; 'white' or 'black' or 'leaden' if there is only one skin colour. Fur is classified into four categories: *vashtu*, when the hair is long and bristly; *tipu*, when it is frizzy; *llambu*, when the hair is straight and unshaped; and, lastly, *tolo* when the hair is scant and frizzy.[7] A tendency to short hair is associated with the fact that this does not hide its body, or disguise its weight, its texture or the quantity of meat; in other words, its thinness is visible. 'Hairy' guinea-pigs are like pets or 'decorations'; people keep no more than one or two of them.

This system of controlling reproduction leaves out one variable which is central to the modern logic of production: the fertility of mothers. Mothers are selected for their age and sexual maturity rather than for their weight or size. People do not isolate mothers which are more fertile from those which are less so. The time of recovery, after delivery, is very short; nor do people give them special food during this period. This means that the level of fertility is generally very low. However, over the year, the more fertile mothers will be marked out from the less fertile ones and the latter used for consumption. In this case, the less fertile *cuya* (the female guinea-pig) is described as *machorra* and *fria* (cold). However, all female guinea-pigs will be killed once they have had three or four deliveries a year. Although there is no unanimous consensus among our informants or veterinary experts, there is an implicit conceptual model of reproduction and practices that go with it.

The number of guinea-pigs kept in a household varies all the time. It is not possible to establish 'rational' systematic control over the number of animals such that the number would be constant or that variations would follow a ritual cycle. As I have argued above, feasts and celebrations are important in determining these quotas. However, once past this number, there are problems of space, of control and especially of feeding. When a group is larger, there is a greater need for care. One major burden is providing a good diet throughout the whole year. This is not simple, because there are periods when there are no good herbage or plants and little alfalfa. We have observed a general decrease in size of the litter during summer from May to September due to the lack of herbage.

The Guinea-pig's Food

The classification of the guinea-pig's food closely follows the logic of 'cold' and 'hot', in both Indian and mestizo communities. The ideal is a combination of herbage and pasture such that the guinea-pigs have a balanced diet. Plants and herbage are therefore classified as 'hotter' or 'colder'. This distinction of degree is very important because, in principle, all the food of the guinea-pig must fall within the category of a symbolic world that excludes complete cold or heat. Hot herbage is better in summer, cold in winter. However, a balance can be achieved through very simple techniques of transformation: cold water and fire are used to transform food from hotter to less hot and from colder to less cold.

Turnips, barley stubble, straw, grass, banana skins, the husks of sweet corn, *ñahui*, cabbage leaves, beans and lentils are among the hottest plants and foodstuffs. In Indian communities, people classify different types of straw according to their thickness and colour. When straw is the main food for guinea-pigs, people choose the greener and softer types. Among those which are regarded as more or less 'fresh' are *chilca*, corn-cob, artemisia and yellow dock. Among the colder ones are *canayuyo* or *quillu sisa, illen, pasto azul, tseleg*, ryegrass and maize leaves. Clearly, many of these plants, grasses or bushes grow in the sierra on fallow land, close to streams, where there is thick vegetation, and close to paths. The classification of these food as 'good' indicates to the member of the family which kinds they should collect during their trips, outings to the market or work in the fields. All these plants have a seasonal cycle of growth. In the sierra, winter is a period of abundance, because pasture and herbage used as fodder grow plentifully. July and August after the harvest are critical months, as well as September and October – just before the time for sowing. Winter is the period in which the number of guinea-pigs decreases, and many of our informants confirmed this. Our data show, on the other hand, that guinea-pigs multiply during the rainy period.

One important distinction needs to be made: the taxonomy of plants and pasture on farmland differs from that of herbage and pasture in the mountains. The former are collected while other crops are growing; the more crops that are available, the less the need to go to the mountains for food. One group of grasses which are considered 'bad' when they grow mixed up with the crops – and therefore compete for soil nutrients – can nevertheless be good food for guinea-pigs. Among these are *nabo*, which grows among barley, and *canayuyo*, which grows among potatoes. In communities where there is plenty of water, the terraced cultivation of potatoes is common. In such cases, *canayuyo* is the main food for guinea-pigs. However, even such 'bad' plants as maize, beans and peas may be used. Many plants regarded as dangerous when growing among cultivated crops are considered suitable food for the guinea-pig. *Chilca*, a kind of small wild shrub which can also be used for fencing, is a very abundant food, and flourishes during the summer. The leaves of beans, lentils and cabbages are regarded as good food too. None the less, alfalfa is considered the ideal food throughout Ecuadorean peasant society. Since this plant was introduced into Ecuador, it has been regarded as the livestock food *par excellence*. Its exceptional nutritional qualities are well known to peasants and, whenever possible, it is cultivated on the edges of fields, especially in the low valleys. One positive aspect of this plant is its exceptional digestive qualities. This is why it is said that even if guinea-pigs eat alfalfa to excess they will never fall ill. So alfalfa is considered to be a tonic for the stomach. For this reason, it should probably be regarded as mainly a medicinal plant, although a distinction between medicinal and nutritional value is not really valid. This becomes clear when informants say that, even in periods of food shortage, it is always desirable to collect new shoots of alfalfa for the guinea-pigs. Moreover, alfalfa is an ideal food for any type of livestock.

As we noted previously, guinea-pigs eat much of the kitchen scraps: barley bran, the peel of soft beans and bananas, slices of cabbage, peel of yellow carrots, onions, maize, pumpkins, courgettes, rotten corn. Guinea-pigs that 'fancy' the leftovers from daily cooking are considered *amañados* (bad-mannered), because they look for this kind of food. None the less, to some extent, this is appreciated, because this kind of diet considerably improves the taste of the meat.

There is no agreement about potato peelings: in some communities, they are considered good food, in others they are believed to be harmful to the stomach. The idea that potato peelings are poisonous is associated with the constant and increasing use of pesticides. People believe that even if potatoes are washed carefully there are chemical residues which are extremely difficult to get rid of completely. But 'bad' plants and herbage are never used as food. Among these are garden spurge, maidenhair fern, yellow clover, dandelion, shave grass, chick-peas, soft oats, nettles and certain types of watercress. These plants are regarded as causes of certain kinds of digestive diseases, which produce intense spasms and culminate with unstoppable diarrhoea. Moreover, people consider the weeds which grow in the wheat fields to be especially dangerous.

As we saw earlier, water is never given to guinea-pigs. This is not only because people think that the quality of the local water is poor. The key idea is that this animal finds it difficult to judge the amount of water it needs to drink, so the best thing is to give water to the animal in the form of herbage and plants. This will prevent it from eating food that is either too dry or too humid. An equilibrium needs to be found in this respect also, and it is a type of knowledge that demands extended practice and extreme care. The act of drying out or soaking grass and herbage is carried out by housewives or grown-up daughters. The feeding of the guinea-pigs twice a day or more is an activity that calls for lot of attention, since an unbalanced diet leads to illnesses. The hot/cold logic which informs diet and health care in the human world is used, analogically, in the animal world too. Eating well means eating with care and with moderation. The quantity of food is increased only at the approach of the period in which guinea-pigs will be slaughtered (or taken to the market). The cultural world of Ecuadorean peasants is a modest world as eating food and drinking to excess are accepted only on exceptional ritual occasions. The analysis of food, then, has now brought us to the subject of illnesses and healing practices.

Sicknesses of Guinea-pigs

The care and the cleanliness of the guinea-pig's habitat are a fundamental priority: the animals are kept in pallets or shelters close to the wall, or in separate hutches, which are usually made with different types of straw (preferably from barley). Straw is also used to construct what is usually called the guinea-pig's 'bed', which prevents the animal from lying in permanent contact with the earth floor of the kitchen. The floor is considered too cold and may cause variations in temperature when the animal sleeps or rests. For similar reasons, it is better to change the straw two or three times a week. By doing so, the urine, the ashes and the leftovers of pasture and plants that the guinea-pigs have eaten are disposed of. Normally, once leftovers have been thrown away, people sweep the pallet and the floor with leaves and with branches of broom.

Broom is a very common perennial bush in the sierra, and produces many wide, thin and straight branches, which are often used to make home-made brooms for sweeping the house. The top part is boiled and used as a laxative or diuretic. It is a common belief that the smell of broom is so strong that it will keep off lice and fleas. The most common technique is to mix leaves or branches of artemisia with barley stubble or with whatever is used to make the pallets.[8]

In some communities, people sprinkle the floor with ashes, after they have done the cleaning, in order to avoid any increase in dampness. This is believed to keep the guinea-pigs warmer. Moreover, people believe that the combination of ashes, plants and grass is very nutritive, and constitutes a good supplement to the normal diet.

One of the priorities and worries of women is also to keep the *chuchuri* at bay to protect the life of the guinea-pig. One practice, which we observed only in some Indian communities, is to boil dried fish with coriander and then wash the floor of the kitchen with the liquor. The idea is that the smell will keep these dangerous animals off, since it is an inauspicious, twice-cold combination.

The guinea-pig, then, is an animal that needs protection and care. Its 'nature' and especially its body and skin are considered to be particularly feeble and frail. A major priority for all the members of the family is to keep the habitat of the guinea-pig at a stable temperature. The skin of the guinea-pig is not as waterproof as that of the rabbit. Therefore, parasites – which we mentioned above – are their worst enemies, especially lice and fleas. In the domestic habitat, the dog is seen as the main transmitter of these parasites. Spraying the kitchen and the guinea-pigs' pallets with insecticide (against flies) is one of the most common 'modern' practices, especially in non-Indian communities. This is done every day during the summer months, when fleas are in great abundance. In Indian communities, at the first sign of fleas in a guinea-pig, people remove the pallets and wash the floor with water mixed with creosote. A new pallet is then made from eucalyptus leaves and branches. Another widespread habit is that of bringing the guinea-pig close to the fire: people believe that fleas and lice 'leap into the fire' because of the effects of the heat. In some cases Malathion (a disinfectant) diluted in water is used to wash the animals.

Obviously, fleas and lice are 'visible' and form part of the environment of the huts. A typical scene in the sierra is the shared task of removing fleas and lice from people's hair, and there is a strong and widespread belief that heat is one of the best remedies for getting rid of them. However, people distinguish *sarna*, which is associated with spots and with the loss of part of the skin, from fleas and lice. *Sarna* is produced by other kinds of external parasites, which do not have a name. They are less visible, but people know that they exist. The most common remedy is the application of paraffin oil to the skin, sometimes mixed with pig fat. Many of our informants admitted that these remedies are not very efficacious, and that, even if the parasites are killed, the paraffin and the fat are strong irritants. In many cases, people know that the best remedy is to wet the animals with warm water, mixed with a preparation that contains some sulphamide.

When people talk about illnesses of guinea-pigs, a set of ideas and opinions emerges about 'catching a cold', 'disease', 'plague', 'fever', 'flu', the appearance of 'bags and tumours' in the skin, 'diarrhoea' and 'swelling'. Sometimes they mention symptoms that can be observed, such as tumours, diarrhoea and swellings, and, in other cases, more general symptoms, such as too high or too low temperature, having a cold (it is believed that guinea-pigs can cough, but this is not certain) or simply disease. In the case of plague, people are thinking about a generalized disease that affects almost the whole group of animals.

There seems to be a certain ambiguity and lack of precision in the identification of the internal diseases that affect guinea-pigs. Experts, veterinary surgeons and rural development workers agree that the traditional remedies are inadequate and incorrect. In my opinion, the main problem is the absence of any clear and convincing classification at the local level, in both the Indian and the other communities. Let me explain this in more detail. The symptoms I have mentioned are, obviously, and perhaps necessarily, widespread. Nevertheless, 'flu', 'swellings' and 'diarrhoea' are associated with a disease that is called *torsón*. It is believed that, when the guinea-pig is struck down by the *torsón*, it walks with a twist as if it has stomach or abdominal pain. 'Swellings' and 'diarrhoea' are very visible symptoms. The cause of this disease is directly related to the guinea-pig's food – whether they have eaten plants which were either too dry or too moist. The balance between cold and hot has therefore been broken. This is the most common disease and cause of death for guinea-pigs.

These symptoms are very similar to those of salmonella: 'weakening, paralysis of the upper arms, diarrhoea, loss of appetite, stomach congestion, inflammation of the liver, the spleen and the kidneys'.[9] This is a bacterial disease, caught via food. Peasants know that this disease is lethal and can be transmitted easily. Their practical transmitted experience enables them to associate it with plants and eating grass but not with 'invisible' bacteria. Obviously, in traditional medicine, the origin of the disease is not related to a classificatory system in which bacteria, viruses and parasites are at the centre of reflection on illness, and, in consequence, the point of departure for medicinal therapies. Nevertheless, both Indian and non-Indian people do talk in general terms about 'microbes'. In that context, the 'diseases of God' or 'microbes' all have an external origin; they come from abroad, in the past from Europe but now from the general environment.[10] All stomach diseases are, in principle, not only 'diseases of God', but also generated by microbes, 'visualized' by our informants as tiny lice, so small that they cannot be seen, and therefore impossible to treat early on, unlike real lice. Therefore they cannot be eliminated in time, as happens with real fleas.[11] The lack of a precise 'scientific' classification prevents peasant women from clearly distinguishing, for instance, salmonella from coccidiosis. The symptoms of coccidiosis are very similar to salmonella, and it is probable that *torsón* covers both these types of disease. The identification of coccidiosis is also difficult for veterinary surgeons without experience, because the presence of diarrhoea can be mistaken for a symptom of salmonella. Veterinary and rural development workers agree that *torsón* as a 'general ailment' is, in the majority of cases, 'native salmonella'.

There is a close connection between this idea and the way diarrhoea is interpreted when it hits children. McKee (1988) differentiates three types of diarrhoea distinguished in popular thought. The first is seen as the product of an infection, due to the presence of bacteria in the environment or as a consequence of ingesting 'heavy meals'. The second is due to a disequilibrium of humours caused by a concentration of heat and cold in the body, while the third is due to supernatural attacks (evil eye, *mal aire* (bad air) and *susto* (fright)). This classification underlies the way people think about diseases of guinea-pigs, even if in an unclear fashion. This is due to the lack of any precise method of classification and to the fact that the taxonomy does not refer to any specific treatment or to any particular kind of expert who ought to be consulted. In the case of human diseases, hypotheses about causes are linked to the type of treatment to be given. But, in the case of animal diseases, there are no veterinary surgeons, healers or 'witch-doctors' to be consulted. The treatment, and eventually the cure, is principally undertaken by women and takes place in their homes.

The diseases mentioned above, attacks by external parasites (fleas and lice), are very similar to *sarna*. Experts agree that these are, without exception, the most common skin diseases. Undoubtedly the local *sarna* is identical with what experts call skin mycosis or external mycosis. In all these cases, there is an invasion of fungus, especially on the head of the guinea-pig. As a matter of curiosity, and contrary to what some experts assume, ticks do not seem to be a common infection among the guinea-pigs.

Now let us return to *torsón* and its therapy. The recommended cure, in some communities, especially in non-Indian ones, is to give pieces or seeds of soft pumpkin to the sick animals. When it is thought that the indigestion is accompanied by 'fever', people mix the pumpkin with herbage, especially with different types of mallow. This therapy is part of Ecuadorean traditional medicine. The properties of the pumpkin are very clear, since it is considered a very effective remedy for curing intestinal parasites (tapeworms), which produce 'swellings', 'weakening' and 'loss of appetite'.[12] In Indian traditional medicine, pumpkin seeds are also used in cases of inflammation of the stomach and diarrhoea.[13] The use of mallow is very common and its properties are also well known in the sierra, the tall and pink mallow being the most frequently used. Both are considered especially efficacious against stomach pains and spasms.[14] Some of our informants pointed out clearly that the association of pumpkin seeds with mallow is very appropriate since it is a combination of something cold – pumpkin seeds – and something hot – the mallow. In parallel with this therapy the question then becomes one of separating sick animals from healthy ones, an operation that is often impossible to carry out when they do not have hutches.

In some Indian communities, *torsón* is called *llancha* or simply *peste* (plague). This last term suggests an external cause of the disease, the symptoms being the same as those analysed above. Mallow and pumpkin seeds are not used, for the most part, on their own. However, we realized that in many cases the idea of 'cleaning' (*limpiada*) the habitat of the guinea-pig is fundamental. Cleaning consists of mixing leaves of artemisia, Santa Maria and plantain with water, and, after it has boiled, sprinkling the liquid on the area where the guinea-pigs live. Later, ashes are sprinkled on to the floor and the guinea-pigs are fed with fresh, mild plants for a few days. In some cases, when ashes are not used, people make a new pallet for the animals, using branches of sprouting eucalyptus when these can be obtained without too much difficulty. Even though there is no direct treatment of the animal's body here, there is a belief that attacks of external 'microbes' can be kept off by using these plants. The use of artemisia is widespread because it is believed to repel fleas. When this plant is put on the floor, or mixed with other herbage, it becomes a repellent.[15] A drink, which is good against bile infection, is also made with the artemisia.[16] Santa Maria is also used as an infusion for curing people suffering from *susto*.[17] The plantain is an evergreen plant frequently used in traditional Ecuadorean medicine and has multiple uses: it cures skin diseases, fever, frequent catarrh and coughs and helps in blood coagulation and the treatment of haemorrhoids.[18] Plantains are also mixed with other herbage such as mulberry, mallow and elderberry to cure inflammation of the stomach and *colerin* (stomach pains which occur together with vomiting).[19] Infusions made from these three plants are considered to be balanced: the plantain, being very cool, should be compensated for by the warmth of the Santa Maria and the artemisia.

Cleansing is mainly a preventive practice, once sick animals have been discovered. The central idea is that the smell prevents the spreading of the disease to other healthy animals. However, this idea coexists with the belief that the smell of the mixture, as well as the leaves of eucalyptus, helps to cure the sick guinea-pigs. This is because microbes flee from the body in the presence of the fumes from the mixed herbage: consequently temperature goes down, and diarrhoea stops. On the other hand, in non-Indian communities, the treatment used is a more direct change of diet. This strategy is also used in some Indian communities, although mixing pumpkin seeds with mallow is never recommended. In these communities, the ideal procedure is to spread mint on the floor. This is done with a double purpose: on the one hand, the smell keeps the microbes off and, on the other, guinea-pigs 'like the taste of mint' and are able to eat it.

Torsón is a disease defined by a series of symptoms described by this specific term. There is no particular analysis of the specific

organs affected, although there is a clear key reference to the
'guts'/'belly'. Both Indian and mestizo people agree on this point.
There is also agreement on the seriousness of the disease, because
of the speed of the infection. This explains the use of the means
of prevention we mentioned above. We have observed discontinuities in peasant knowledge and in traditional practices: Indian
people are less concerned about changing the diet of guinea-pigs.
However, it is important to point out the continuity between
knowledge of plants and herbage and their use for both human
beings and animals. As an example, it is sufficient to mention
pumpkin seeds, which are frequently used in traditional Indian
medicine. This 'local veterinary science' is a field of experimentation in which the limits between different types of living beings
are not sharply defined. At this level, obviously, it is in complete
accord with the principle of 'modern or universal veterinary
science', which also attempts to establish common therapies for
human beings and animals on the basis of a principle of unity
between the body and its functions. Salmonella is also a disease
that afflicts human beings, and its modern treatment simply
involves the supply of a certain doses of sulphamide and antibiotics
diluted in water for a period of between five and seven days.[20] Our
informants consider that the remedies used are efficacious
although they concede that, in many cases, mortality in the group
is very high. Obviously one of the main problems is that in the
traditional treatment of these diseases it is very difficult to separate
sick from healthy animals. However, we have observed that very
sick animals are killed and buried or thrown away far from the
houses, in order to avoid the spread of infection. Moreover, it
is a common practise to avoid introducing new animals into a
group which has been affected by the 'plague'. I do not want to
embark on a discussion about the different degrees of efficacy of
traditional and modern treatments, only to point out that local
veterinary ideas are complex and that there are therefore a variety
of practices that originate from global ideas about health and
sickness. Our approach, via the guinea-pig, necessarily draws us
towards the wider world of traditional medicine.

Let us now look at one of the most common diseases among
guinea-pigs beside *torsón*. It is known as a 'chill' (*frío*), as 'cooling'
(*enfriamiento*) or 'flu' (*gripes*). Its cause can be of two kinds: sudden
changes of temperature and/or the presence of microbes, seen in
concrete terms as lice. Some of the symptoms are like those of

salmonella, particularly high temperature and general weakening, but with the further additions of frequent sneezing and violent shaking of the head. These often occur together with severe diarrhoea. The general conception is that the guinea-pig, being a weak animal, has 'lazy' intestines. In our talks with informants, a further important aspect emerged: the 'cries' and 'groans' of the guinea-pig. As we have pointed out, our informants believed that these cries and groans can sometimes be mistaken for *torsón*. In order to distinguish between those two sicknesses, people often refer to the 'words' of the guinea-pig: when a guinea-pig has a cold or flu, it is said to produce a noise similar to the sound 'sh' and, in the case of *torsón*, to the human sound 'uy'. The first treatment, obviously, is to control the temperature and to produce a lot of smoke on the first day on which an animal is found to be affected by the disease. Many informants claim that a hot and dry hutch is the best cure. This process lasts between three and five days. Likewise, people change the pallets regularly, using fresh branches. In some non-Indian communities, the same diet of pumpkin seeds and mallow is used as that used in cases of salmonella. In Indian communities, the mixture of the three plants is also used. Those practices indicate that, even if the illnesses are different, the treatments are similar. In principle, these remedies are employed together with the separation of sick from healthy animals. There is a general belief, confirmed by experience, that young animals fall ill more often than adult ones. Pregnant females come second. Hence, special care and attention are paid to these animals.

Apart from specific therapies, there is special concern for the diet of sick animals. Normally the diet is a regular one, depending on the availability of plants and grasses. Normally people do not waste much time looking for what is regarded as ideal food for guinea-pigs. However, more attention is paid to their diet when they are ill; in periods of sickness, their diet is changed; special care is taken with drying and humidifying the food, and, whenever possible, the quantity of food is checked to avoid overheating. These precautions indicate a concern for avoiding possible causes of changes of temperature and 'microbes', especially lice, which are generally believed to transmit nearly all the diseases. This type of care goes hand in hand with preventive measures and direct cures by means of diet.

I mentioned above animals which are enemies of the guinea-pig. When people talk about a swelling of the belly which is not *torsón*

– in other words, a light diarrhoea that is easy to control – they usually attribute this to the fact that the guinea-pig has eaten grass mixed with the urine of toads. Some of our informants explained that pregnant guinea-pigs sometimes have miscarriages. This is because of the *susto* created – in our informants' words – by the presence of 'strangers' in the house, by other animals entering the shelter and, even worse, by intuitions about the proximity of a *chuchuri* (the most feared animal). This relates to the idea that the guinea-pig is a timid animal, in need of protection. Its shyness is so notorious that an informant told us that a guinea-pig is 'too stupid to be left outside'. Obviously the idea of *susto* or *espanto* (fright) refers to illnesses 'of the land' as opposed to 'illnesses of God', to which I have previously referred and which are common in rural Ecuador. It is interesting that this idea about the guinea-pig exists, but that nothing can ever be done, since it is only a matter of providing a *post factum* explanation of an irreversible event, such as a miscarriage. The only possible measure is preventive: to avoid the presence of strangers in the house and, obviously, to keep away animals which are enemies of guinea-pigs.

Visible and Bland Meat

I hope that I have demonstrated that a 'common culture' of the guinea-pig exists, and that the variations between Indian and non-Indian ideas and practices are not so great as to create a sharp contrast between different productive worlds. Moreover, religious variations are not particularly significant. In Palmira Dávalos, the traditional production of guinea-pigs still exists, despite the fact that it competes with ideas about hygiene that have been introduced recently. For our female producers, the main objective of their production strategy is the production of what I would call 'visible' meat, in other words the production of a healthy and fat guinea-pig. Hence, we would expect to find sophisticated knowledge about the ideal diet and the health of the guinea-pig. The genetic model advocated by development workers might give rise to significant improvements, but this would imply a change in the traditional management of the guinea-pig.

In local eyes, a 'fat' guinea-pig is an animal that weighs more than 600 grams, a weight that can be reached under normal conditions of production with a normal, traditional work input.

What is important to remember above all else is that 'visible meat' should not be converted into 'everyday' meat. Our female producers in a society in which the normal diet is basically vegetarian have no interest in maximizing the production of 'cheap and fatless' protein. If we were dealing with social actors who were involved in 'the hunt for protein', the productive scenario would be different. I cannot, therefore, even assess the real importance of the guinea-pig as a source of protein in the communities we have studied. So the analysis of Bolton and Calvin (1981), based on the idea that people eat guinea-pigs because of protein shortage, is both right and wrong.[21] It is true in so far as guinea-pigs are a source of protein, and it is wrong, because, if the objective were to maximize protein consumption (assuming the truth of the hypothesis that the normal diet manifests an evident lack of balance), they would have to produce more animals, and this does not happen, for reasons which are 'culturally patterned'. The tendency, rather, is to keep between ten and fifteen guinea-pigs to be consumed on appropriate occasions; intensification of production in particular periods depends on variations in weather, feed, the presence or absence of plague and, mainly, the requirements of the festival calendar and the less predictable cycle of social and moral obligations. We have, nevertheless, recorded periods and families with very few guinea-pigs.

In this productive context, along with the health and the fatness of the guinea-pigs, taste is an important value in the production of meat. Producers are especially concerned with producing a tasty, distinctive meat, fit for slaughter. This requires paying attention to the smoking, the balance between hot and cold and the choice of the best diet for the guinea-pig. Concern for the temperature of the habitat, grass and plants (neither too dry nor too clammy, in other words neither too hot nor too cold) and for health care are ideas that are central to an understanding of their concern with taste: guinea-pig meat needs to be bland, because this is a guarantee of a good taste. There is an evident culinary passion about guinea-pigs, which we shall examine in the next chapter.

Notes

1. The problem of what constitutes 'meat' might seem a stupid question since we could just take the consistency of the animal's flesh as an adequate criterion. However, we know that there are different types of 'meat': some are redder, others whiter, others fattier or leaner. In Ecuadorean culture, it is fundamental to ask about 'heat', as there is 'hotter' or 'colder' meat. Vialles (1987), in his beautiful and 'horrific' book about the slaughterhouses of Adour in France, has shown that we cannot obtain 'meat' without going through the act of killing a specific type of animals which are edible. Animals that have died a natural death, either because of disease or from an accident, are not normally eaten, simply because they have not been slaughtered. In order to eat meat, it is necessary and essential to see blood flowing. In modern society, the act of killing animals has become the exclusive task of specialists and takes place in aseptic sites, away from public view. Consumers have access only to a 'purified' meat and are removed from the horrific sight of the killers. In rural Ecuador, the slaughter and the separation of the meat from the blood is still a domestic activity. Children participate in the act as spectators until they are old enough to perform it themselves. Eating guinea-pig in Ecuador thus implies taking an active role in the killing of the animal. Later, we shall come back to this issue when we note that guinea-pig meat is not bought in butchers' shops or in supermarkets.
2. As a general introduction to the guinea-pig, see especially King (1956), Gade (1957), Luna de la Fuente and Moreno Rojas (1969), Chivilchez Chávez (1980) and Zevallos (1980). For an introduction to the animals of the Andes see Wing (1975).
3. Guamán Poma de Ayala (1956, p. 174) recorded that more than a thousand guinea-pigs and hundreds of llamas were slaughtered and offered to the gods in Cuzco as an auspicious act designed to influence the coming harvest. Polo de Ondegardo (1916, p. 37) discussed the importance of the guinea-pig in divination.
4. In Indian culture, toads are associated with black magic and are often used to do harm (see Aguiló, 1987, p. 29). Their presence is disturbing and considered a sign of bad luck. Among non-Indian peasants, toads are feared, and the idea of eating them is seen as something ultimately horrific. Bolton and Calvin write that one of their informants argues 'that old guinea-pigs turn into toads, and grow tails and run about grunting like toads' (1981, p. 289). This belief does not seem to be so widespread in Ecuador.
5. Bolton and Calvin found that 'smoke is also considered to be an element for the well-being of the guinea-pig, and many peasants think that without smoke guinea-pigs cannot survive. It is believed that

litters and pregnant females are more likely to die if they are not reared in a smoky habitat' (1981, p. 279). Likewise they observe that for many informants 'guinea-pigs do not need to drink because they drink smoke'. Smoke is their 'drink' (1981, p. 279). Escobar and Escobar have also found this belief over the whole Cuzco region (1972, p. 37). I agree with this interpretation, because the meaning of 'smoke' is a wider one, and refers not only to smoke produced by the fireplace, but also to that produced by cooking and boiling. Therefore, 'drinking smoke' is associated with the idea of steam. This is also Bolton and Calvin's line of interpretation. Hence smoke maintains a certain temperature in the habitat, and this temperature has to be 'balanced' in terms of suitable humidity.

6. *Malta* is a Quechua word which means middle-sized. The term *malton* is a Hispanicism. In non-Indian communities, the classification is simple: young animals, adults and, among them, fertile and infertile ones and, lastly, the old.

7. Colour and texture of the hair seem to be the most common criteria of classification of guinea-pigs in other Andean contexts (see Bolton and Calvin, 1981, pp. 261–71; Luna de la Fuente and Moreno Rojas, 1969, p. 31). In Colombia, the presumed region or place of origin is added to the colour and texture of the hair. Out of these combinations, there are sixteen different types (see Castaño Quintero, 1981, pp. 8–17). If we had restricted our focus in Ecuador to colour alone, we would undoubtedly have found a great quantity of different types of guinea-pigs.

8. Artemisia is a native Ecuadorean plant frequently used in traditional medicine. White has noticed that people use infusions of this herb to combat pain during menstrual periods, and its juice as a preventive against internal abscesses. The plant kills or at least keeps off fleas (1982, p. 202). Moreover, he adds that broom is another native plant which has multiple applications: against vomiting, as a laxative, a diuretic and an emetic (1982, p. 256).

9. See Sousa and Chalampuente, 1980, p. 14.

10. This distinction between 'diseases of the land' and 'diseases of God' is central to Indian medical thought. Eduardo Estrella (1978) argues that the former have a 'supernatural' origin, while the latter are always linked to 'natural' phenomena. Muñoz Bernand (1986) has also found this distinction among the Indian people of Pindilig. 'Diseases of God' are associated with the penetration of white people into Indian territory and with the deterioration of social relations. Smallpox, infectious diseases of children, typhoid, plague, tuberculosis, alcoholism and lying in after birth are considered to be caused by 'microbes' (or as punishments sent by God) (1986, p. 65). Muñoz Bernand has also pointed out that 'diseases of the land' are specifically Indian diseases. They are considered to be ancient sick-

nesses, generated from 'before the Conquest', and include wind sickness (*mal aire*), *mal viento* or *mala visión* (bad eyesight), the 'rainbow' and the sickness caused by mountains that are hard to climb. I shall come back to these issues later.

11. See Muñoz Bernand (1986, p. 66).
12. White points out that pumpkin seeds are very nutritious and are used in traditional medicine to cure worms and more recently, tapeworms (1982, pp. 313–14). Adriana Bianchi has pointed out that in Cotopaxi people use pumpkin seeds to deal with and cure attacks of worms and tapeworms (1986, p. 19).
13. See Bianchi (1986, p. 21) and Acero Coral and Pianalto de Dalle Rive (1985, p. 60).
14. Bianchi (1986) mentions that the scented mallow is particularly good for stomach illnesses and the white mallow for liver afflictions. White distinguishes three types of mallow: the tall one, used for bronchial ailments, lung congestion and stomach inflammation; the white mallow, used for coughs, catarrh and as eye drops in case of eye irritation; and the pink, used as a mouth rinse and against ear pains (1982, pp. 194–8). Muñoz Bernand only mentions the scented mallow. This plant is considered to be hot, and is taken as an infusion against *mal aire* (1986, p. 44).
15. See White (1982, p. 202). There are many parallels with the logic of ritual 'cleansing' in cases of diarrhoea, described by McKee (1988, pp. 222–3). The idea of cleansing is to take the 'disease' out of the sick person. This is also possible by rubbing the body with strong-smelling objects. The disease will then be attracted by the smell. McKee mentions, among other things, the following sweet-smelling herbage: *chilca*, feverfew, *guantug*, *paracon yuyu* and artemisia. As we have seen, the majority of these are used for cleansing of the guinea-pigs, too.
16. See Bianchi (1986, p. 17).
17. Muñoz Bernand (1986, p. 46) writes that this hot herb 'is given to people who are suffering from *susto* as an infusion, together with pennyroyal and grapefruit'. She also points out that this plant is used for the *mal viento* (1986, p. 46). Bianchi also mentions that it is used to cure *espanto* and the evil eye (1986, p. 35).
18. See White (1982, pp. 191–2).
19. See Bianchi (1986, p. 21) and Muñoz Bernand (1986, p. 43).
20. This treatment is recommended by Luna de la Fuente and Moreno Rojas (1969, p. 76) and Sousa and Chalampuente (1980, p. 15).
21. Bolton and Calvin write:

    We will show that the people of Santa Bárbara do not eat guinea-pig because there is a feast, but instead they celebrate the main festivals when there is guinea-pig meat to eat. The celebrations do not lead to the sacrifice of the guinea-pigs; those are sacrificed because of the need for protein in the diet and because of the condition of the animals just before the celebration (1981, p. 305).

CHAPTER FOUR

The Meat Transformed

We have seen that the main concern of the women is to produce, first of all, a healthy and fat animal. Their knowledge and their productive practices lead them to try to strike a balance between the quantity of the guinea-pigs and the quality of the food, and between a 'pure and healthy' reproduction and 'ideal' conditions of hygiene and health. Hence health and food care require special attention and a body of knowledge and understanding which is transmitted in the family. Even if daughters are the depositaries of this knowledge, male spouses and children also help in collecting 'good food' whenever it can be found, as when they go to the fields. The production of guinea-pigs is therefore a family task.

The 'fate' of the guinea-pig is to be turned into food. It is therefore a part of the universe available for disposal, to be transformed into a source both of life and of pleasure. It is a source of life because its proteins become energy, a source of pleasure because eating guinea-pig is enjoyable. The choice of the guinea-pig as a 'meal', and its preparation, will receive particular attention in this chapter. As already mentioned, we need to ask not only why the guinea-pig becomes a food, but what the rules of transformation are – in other words, to study the 'recipe book' for guinea-pigs, as well as the contexts in which this transformation can take place. This latter idea is very simple: generally we do not eat on our own; we gather with other people to eat on particular occasions. Hence, the act of eating implies the observation of different types of protocol which must be complied with by the social actors and which have to be understood by an observer.

The guinea-pig holds a special place as an 'exceptional food' in the context of the Ecuadorean peasant culture and economy, which suffers from periodic shortages of domestic food production. This economy, therefore, requires fixed and permanent cash inputs and the guinea-pig has a role of 'exceptional meal'. Producing guinea-pigs – which are then consumed – brings the producers merit and is associated with a certain kind of 'culinary' prestige and pride. Our informants systematically and continuously emphasize the importance of the 'taste' of the meat in the relationship between the habitat of the guinea-pig, smoke, the fire, proximity to the fireplace and the ideal 'smoked' taste. I am not overstating the matter when I point out that raising guinea-pigs involves a special contact, a kind of immersion in a 'meat' which is produced in an intimate way. Our informants know that every litter is destined to be slaughtered, its maturity depending upon proper food or healthy conditions. In this way, a fat and healthy guinea-pig – one which, in consequence, has tasty meat – tells us a great deal about the quality of care given to it by its owner; as part of her daily activity, a 'material substance' becomes crystallized as food.

The production and transformation of guinea-pigs are two distinct processes in time, both involved in the social appropriation of nature. Obviously, the slaughtering of a guinea-pig is conceived of as its logical and foreseen end. Before anything else, the guinea-pig has been and will always be food. This demands its death and ritual consumption. Guinea-pigs have no name, and are marked out only by their colour, hair, age and sex. They belong to a particular category and are an abstraction, despite their proximity to and their cohabitation with humans. In this cultural world, therefore, there is no space for being sorry for oneself or feeling any sense of guilt at having slaughtered a specific individual. I hope that the above-mentioned issues will become clearer throughout this chapter.

The Value of Guinea-pig Meat

In all our conversations and field notes, guinea-pig meat was highly prized and was always described as the 'best' meat when compared with other domestic, edible and highly regarded meat: lamb, goat, beef, pork and chickens. So why is it the best? In the first place, its 'taste' and 'flavour' are emphasized. People insist on its 'sweetness' and its smoky taste. Both Indians and mestizos agree that guinea-pig meat is 'sweeter' than other meat, and even say that it is 'sweeter than pork'. Here 'flavour' is clearly associated with the fact of being 'sweet'. In the distinction between the sweet and the salty in peasant culture – and in Ecuadorean culture generally – the 'sweet' is always seen as more flavoursome than the salty. The idea of sweetness is also associated with the ideas of 'pleasure' and 'satisfaction', and arises when people argue about the best kinds of potatoes or which kind of maize is the 'sweeter'. So a 'sugary' taste is an ideal aspect of 'flavour' and 'taste'.[1]

The importance of smoke seems to be linked to certain conceptions which contrast dry and salty meat with smoked meat – even if the latter technique is used as much as the former. Obviously, in the case of the guinea-pig, smoke is conceived as something that transmits a certain type of taste to the meat in the process of breeding, without any actual smoking process taking place. But there is clearly another association, on the one hand, between drying and salting and, on the other, between smoking and not salting. It is common in rural Ecuador to think that smoke is not 'dry' and thus preserves the 'humidity' of the meat.

We can infer, then, a set of ideas about the 'ideal state' of meat, in other words those points in time at which it has undergone the necessary 'ripening' – when the 'flavour' has acquired its definite character. Our female informants are clear and categorical about this: guinea-pigs have to be eaten while still young, *maltones*, and not when they are old. Tasty meat is young with plenty of flesh, one informant said. We shall see later that old meat, past its best, can also be eaten, but, if so, will be used to make a stew. Young meat, though, is best roasted.

Another characteristic, not related to taste, but to a certain intrinsic, odourless and 'invisible' characteristic, is the 'heat' of the meat. In the logic of hot and cold, the guinea-pig is ranked higher than pork, lamb, beef and goat meat. The idea of 'heat' is firstly associated with the generation of energy, and secondly with other qualities; it is considered, for instance, to be 'pure' and 'nutritious'. These last two aspects become salient when guinea-pig meat is compared with other meats – especially with pork, a meat also considered very 'hot'. Pork, though 'hot', is less pure and nutritious, and is 'fatter' and 'heavier'. Consequently, a pure and nutritious food is easily assimilable and digestible.

In every community except Chismaute the guinea-pig's 'hot' quality was regarded as superior to that of pork and beef. In Chismaute, on the contrary, people believe that lamb is hotter than pork or meat from cows. One of the explanations of this difference pertains to consumption rather than just to abstract conceptualizations. The mode of consumption – in other words, eating practices – can undoubtedly influence and condition the hierarchies we have pointed out. From empirical observation in Chismaute, people consume more lamb than in other communities. However, despite these differences, the guinea-pig does not lose its central place in the Andean classificatory system.[2]

Within this continuum, the coldest meats are chicken and rabbit, which are thought of as 'lean' and 'thin'. In conversations with informants, when we tried to point out a logical difference since these qualities were associated with 'purity' and the 'nutritive value' of the guinea-pig, they were perplexed because they recognized some discontinuity in the classificatory system. But the typical argument – that 'things are just like that, full stop' – tends to conceal one factor which is very evident to an observer: that the ceremonial role of guinea-pig meat is not only physical but also social, particularly values associated with the generation of social relations. Here I am thinking particularly of ritualized social relations. I shall come back to this aspect later in this chapter.[3]

Another way of conceptualizing heat and cold – in an open-ended and perhaps hypothetical way – is to imagine possible combinations of different kinds of meat. For some of our informants, it is possible to make *secos* (stews of various kinds) by combining different types of meat, for instance, pork, lamb, guinea-pig or chicken. In no case, though, is it possible to mix guinea-pig and pork. Here, the 'logic of energy' triumphs over the 'logic of purity': there is no place for two raw, hot substances, even if one has no fat at all, as is the case with the guinea-pig meat. I conclude then, that the 'logic of energy' is in the main arbitrary, and therefore a 'cultural' product *par excellence*. However, this empirical peasant logic has correspondences with an empirical scientific logic: the protein content, gram for gram, of guinea-pig meat is higher than for any other kind of meat.[4]

The Slaughtering of the Guinea-pig

Once it is decided that a guinea-pig is going to be eaten, it has to be slaughtered. The person in charge of slaughtering the animals is the female 'head of the family', sometimes helped by her older daughters. The technique used in slaughtering guinea-pigs is said to influence the flavour and the taste of the meat. Let us examine this more closely. Different types of slaughtering techniques are said to 'produce a quick death' or to ensure that the animal does not suffer, or 'that the meat keeps its flavour'. The most common method is death by suffocation. One of the most widespread ways it is to take the animal in one's hands, leaning it against one arm, with the other hand tightening its snout so as to prevent it from breathing. Another way is to force the head against the heart and twist it suddenly. This operation, a form of death by asphyxia, has to be done quickly and sharply; the sharp noise which results means that the neck bones have been broken.[5] Our informants agreed that these are the best ways, since the animal 'dies peacefully', and keeps its 'flavour' if bled immediately by splitting it with a knife and hanging it in the open for a few minutes. Later the entrails are removed.

Other methods of slaughter, less often used, are more violent; hitting the guinea-pig on the head with a stone, or simply smashing its nose and then its head on the floor or against a rock. Female informants were familiar with all these techniques, but none practise them, because they are regarded as too 'inhuman', 'very violent' and 'cause the little animal suffering'. All agree that these extreme ways of slaughter cause blood to be 'spilt inside the body', producing, in consequence, 'a bad taste in the meat'. Although people talk about this flavour, which obviously nobody has ever tasted, they nevertheless believe that it exists on the grounds that 'people told them that it loses its sweetness'. It would appear that the existence of these ideas and the fact that slaughtering of this kind, at the hands of someone unknown to them, has the function of differentiating between a 'good death' and a 'bad death'. Slaughtering an animal and eating it imply giving it a death that from both a human and a culinary point of view is the kindest possible. Undoubtedly, some of our informants agree to accept killing by rubbing or twisting the animal, but only when the guinea-pig is then roasted. Apparently, the taste is not damaged and can even 'improve' when the animal is roasted. However, people agree that making a broth or a soup out of guinea-pig meat that has been killed in this way is not allowed, because 'the meat is spoiled'.

Once bled and the guts removed, the animal is skinned.[6] The techniques involved are simple. Hot water is poured over the animal while it is being skinned, or it may be soaked several times in boiling water. In other cases, it is left for some time in boiling water until the skin is soft. It can then be removed very easily. 'Skinning' is an exclusively manual and female operation. Although the slaughter can be a shared task in which men may help, the actual peeling off of the skin is a female chore.

Once the guinea-pig is skinned, it is washed several times with warm water. This is called the 'cleaning' of the guinea-pig. Special attention is paid to washing the anus carefully. After this operation, the animal is ready to be cooked. However, it is normal to let it hang for some time, as is also done with birds and rabbits. The idea is that the guinea-pig has to 'take the air', and that the meat needs to begin drying before being 'worked' and eventually cut into pieces.

Recipes for Guinea-pig Meat

In the previous sections, I pointed out how sets of rules and social conventions define what is food and therefore influence which kinds of raw food can be combined as specific 'dishes'. In addition to food taboos, which specify what it is possible to eat and what not, further unpredictable transformations occur – a sort of 'enigma' and 'mystery' – which do not allow one to predict the 'recipes' that are involved. 'Recipes', in consequence, are dynamic and creative aspects of cooking, whether 'local' or 'international', and are the basis of certain types of knowledge and culinary practices that make it possible for an observer to study the different contexts of food consumption. So recipes are always linked to the type of food and to certain types of social events. Since these events are mainly social occasions, we can hypothesize that, in principle, there will be a certain homology between types of food and recipes and certain types of social relations. Leach (1970) has pointed out that, from an anthropological perspective, what is interesting is to discover empirically those types of food which are treated with particular respect, thereby establishing the logic of different levels of social status and unveiling implicit and explicit hierarchies in the social order.[7] In this section I shall focus on recipes. Later I shall come back to events and occasions.

The universal validity of Lévi-Strauss's culinary triangle has been discussed extensively and I do not intend to go into this debate.[8] Rather I use some of his ideas in order to systematize my analysis of guinea-pig cooking. Lévi-Strauss (1965, 1968) argues that food is presented to people in three different forms: raw, cooked or rotten.[9] The raw obviously constitutes a spotless and pure state, while the other conditions involve transformative processes: the cooked as cultural transformations of the raw, and the rotten as natural transformations. In this way, the triangle of the cooked, the raw and the rotten delimits an 'external' semantic field. Obviously, any cooking privileges particular cultural practices. Nothing is simply cooked, since cooking has to be done in a certain way. In other words, food does not exist in some pure state, since it is normally washed and chopped. If we accept this reasoning – which is explicit in Lévi-Strauss – it is interesting to examine how the raw is transformed into the cooked. Lévi-Strauss firstly makes a distinction between roasting and boiling, roasting being a special technique of the act of 'cooking'. The choice between these, in my opinion, is central to an understanding not only of culinary variations about cooking guinea-pigs, but also for achieving a better understanding of peasant Ecuadorean cooking in general. Let me explain this in more detail.

Lévi-Strauss argues that when food is roasted there is a direct relationship with fire, while when it is boiled there is a twofold process of mediation, firstly through water – in which the guinea-pigs are soaked – and secondly through the use of the vessel which contains them.[10] The act of roasting is therefore a more 'natural' act than the act of boiling – which needs both some kind of vessel and the mediation of water and fire. Lévi-Strauss points out that the act of roasting is a sort of 'exogenous' cooking, given to 'strangers', while boiled food is a sort of 'endogenous' cooking, given to members of the family. Likewise, he suggests, boiling is a way of conserving the nutritional properties of food, since everything is retained, whereas in roasting there is a major loss of nutrients. Boiling is therefore both an economic and a democratic cultural practice, in the sense of being a common rural practice, while roasting is, fundamentally, an act which shows generosity and an aristocratic approach.[11] Boiling and roasting consequently entail differences of status among individuals and social classes. This needs to be discussed in further detail.

Lévi-Strauss uses three indicators: the type of fire, the presence or absence of water and the use or lack of use of a vessel. When people boil food, fire is used directly, although in reality the direct contact is with the vessel, the casserole or the pan, which is full of water. Obviously, fire and water are both needed. When food is roasted, though, fire is also used directly, but there are no vessels and no need for water. This means:

Boiling: Direct fire (+): Vessel (+): Water (+)
Roasting: Direct fire (+): Vessel (–): Water (–)

There are, however, other transformative techniques in use in Ecuador, notably frying and baking.[12] In frying, a further element is introduced which has not been present hitherto in our analysis: the use of fats and oils. The use of an oven, not only for baking bread but also for preparing meat, implies another type of fire, which, for want of a better term, I shall call 'radiant' – in other words the use of indirect fire in contrast to its use in boiling, roasting or frying. One obvious example is the preparation of baked pork – a delicate and much appreciated way of preparing this meat. *Cebiche*,[13] another national dish, introduces a complication, since it is a way of cooking fish and certain types of shellfish without using fire, but with the mediation of lemon. In this respect, we might consider *cebiche* as a variation – excellent in taste and texture – of techniques used in order to reach a point in 'rotting' close to actual cooking. Obviously, from an Indian point of view, *cebiche* is fish and shellfish cooked in lemon and not 'rotted' in lemon.

These additional criteria allow us, therefore, to construct the following classification:

Boiling: Direct fire (+): Vessel (+): Water (+): Fat (–)
Roasting: Direct fire (+): Vessel (–): Water (–): Fat (–)
Frying: Direct fire (+): Vessel (+): Water (–): Fat (+)
Baking: Direct fire (–): Vessel (–): Water (–): Fat (–)

So a 'dish' is normally a combination of various operations, in which some components may be fried and others roasted.

Consequently it is possible to suggest that the result – from the point of view of taste and presentation – is what matters. It is important to remember that in every empirical analysis we need to differentiate the main component – in this case, guinea-pig meat – from secondary ones. I therefore focus on the way on which guinea-pig meat is prepared in order to see whether it should be considered to be roasted or a dish cooked otherwise.

Guinea-pig meat in Ecuador, in the communities we have studied, is prepared by using four techniques of transformation, which we have already mentioned: it may be roasted, fried, boiled or baked. Undoubtedly, roast guinea-pig is the 'dish of kings' *par excellence*.

The views of our informants, both men and women, adolescents and old people, are naturally not Lévi-Straussian. They do not contrast this 'aristocratic and noble' kind of cooking with other, more vulgar ones. They simply observe that the meat has more taste; that the temperature is better maintained; that it can be served in one piece; or that its quality can be seen ('the quality of the "little" animal is very visible because it is not cut into pieces'); and that it takes a long time to prepare ('roasting guinea-pig is hard work'). Other forms of cooking come lower down in the hierarchy. Baking guinea-pig, however, is not very common, since it is fairly unusual to have an oven in the house, especially in Indian communities. Frying guinea-pig is a quick way of preparing it, and does not require a long process of marination. There are different ideas, though, about boiling guinea-pig meat: in some communities this is common; in others it is considered a poor way of cooking, because the 'meat is slimy'. Let us start our culinary journey with the practice of roasting guinea-pig meat.

Roast Guinea-pig

In order to keep what is called the 'gleam' of this dish, it is necessary to marinate it a day ahead. There are several different dressings, but I mention only a few used in recipes for cooking two or three big guinea-pigs (around 800 grams):

> 2 red onions, roughly chopped
> 4 cloves of garlic, finely chopped
> cumin (2 teaspoons)
> one teaspoonful of white pepper
> salt (approximately two teaspoonsful for each animal)
> 2 tablespoonfuls of water
> 2 tablespoonfuls of oil
> annatto as colouring
>
> Mix all the ingredients well and spread them both on the inside and the outside of the animal. Instead of oil, lard with annatto may be used.

A variant of this dressing has been given to us in the community of Guzo. In addition to the ingredients mentioned above, water and oil are replaced with *chicha de jora* (germinated maize), which gives a particularly appetizing taste to the meat. This variant, though not mentioned in other communities, is probably known elsewhere, too.

Before roasting the guinea-pig, it is necessary to remove any excess dressing from the previous day to avoid burning the meat. The animal is roasted on charcoal, on a stick, preferably at its extremity, so that it can be turned without burning. The animal is thus spitted on the stick inserted in the back part, the anal region, and exiting from the jaw. Once spitted on the stick, the usual technique is to tie the front feet and stretch the legs. Once it is stretched out, it is put on a grill or in a basin. During roasting, lard is spread over it to avoid drying out the meat. The guinea-pig is ready when the skin is almost ready to burst.

Despite the addition of the dressing and the lard, guinea-pig meat is very light and may then become hard and chewy. Roasted guinea-pig is therefore traditionally eaten with peanut sauce. Among many recipes, this is my favourite:

> 2 tablespoons of lard
> annatto colouring
> 2 white onions, finely chopped
> 2 cloves of garlic
> salt
> a pinch of cumin
> 1 large cup of roasted and ground coffee with peanuts
> 3½ cups of milk
>
> Fry the onions until they turn golden brown. While they are cooking prepare peanuts mixed with milk, and then pour it over the frying onions. Then cook the mixture at low heat for a good half-hour. If the sauce is too thick, add a bit of milk at the end.

Obviously, roast guinea-pig has to be served with other things. There are various possibilities, but the most common is to serve it with boiled potatoes and chillies. Coriander is normally chopped over the top of the boiled potatoes. Another popular variation is to serve the meat with *tostados* (grilled maize), or simply to add potatoes. The guinea-pig is also served up, especially in mestizo communities, with slices of fresh cheese and a few beans. During our fieldwork, we observed the growing importance of rice as an accompaniment to many meals, especially among mestizo peasants. Using rice usually means less potatoes and maize. In some places, roast guinea-pig with rice is called *seco*.

One of the most common alternatives to pure peanut sauce is the *runaucho* – a sort of *colada* – which accompanies pieces of roast guinea-pig. This is a very delicate dish and can be eaten also with other roast meats. The recipe, which has many variations, begins with frying the following ingredients:

2 tablespoonfuls of pork fat
annatto colouring
2 chopped white onions
2 cloves of garlic
a pinch of cumin
white pepper to taste

When this mixture has been fried, salt is added to taste, plus nearly two litres of water. Then add the following:

one cup of mild oats
20 *cholas* – peeled potatoes

Let the mixture cook for a good half-hour or until the potatoes are ready. Then remove the potatoes and put them on one side. Care has to be taken that the sauce does not become too thick. If this happens, add a little water or milk.

Then prepare half a cup of peanuts with half a litre of milk, which is added to the broth. After a few minutes, mix a large cup of bean flour with half a litre of milk (preferably warm) and add it to the broth. Leave it to cook on a very low heat for nearly half an hour, stirring constantly to avoid the sauce sticking to the bottom of the pan. Just before serving, it is advisable to add a bit of coriander and oregano or, if preferred, just coriander. The *runaucho* is poured on the potatoes, which are served with a generous piece of guinea-pig.

Roast guinea-pig is also called *ají de cuy*. This dish is normally made on a base of onions and tomatoes, together with peanut sauce, and includes some of the giblets, such as the heart, the liver and the kidneys. We have noticed that only on exceptional occasions are the entrails used, since washing them requires a lot

of patience because of their small size. Our informants agree on
the importance of eliminating any taste of excrement when they
cook the entrails, which are carefully washed many times with water
and salt, to which a good quantity of mint has been added. Those
used are extremely finely chopped. In Palmira Dávalos, this
dressing – mixed with the usual peanut sauce – is called *menestra*.
It is worth while mentioning another variant of the *ají de cuy*.
This is when the dish is served with boiled potatoes or half-cooked
yuccas. It is customary in certain places – especially in mestizo
communities – to boil potatoes with the roasted head of the guinea-
pig. This process is a refinement which gives the potatoes a special
taste. Likewise, peanut sauce is often replaced as a base by a sauce
of pumpkin seeds, made with the usual fried onions and tomatoes
plus two cups of milk. This dish is served with colourful and hot
chillies and, if available, two boiled and shelled eggs as decoration.

Fried Guinea-pig

For the majority of our female informants, guinea-pig meat is fried
when there is no time to roast it. In any case, it is advisable to keep
it in a marinade for at least a few hours or to fry it after marinating.
The same sauce is used which we described when talking about
roast guinea-pig. This dressing is undoubtedly the most commonly
used when roasting, baking or frying guinea-pig meat. When
guinea-pig is fried, normally in lard, people usually also fry onions
and sometimes a little garlic. Fried guinea-pig is usually served with
white rice (especially in mestizo communities), or with potatoes
or *mote* (boiled maize), and, obviously, chillies.

In order to fry guinea-pig meat, the animal has to be chopped
into pieces. The most common way of cutting it up is as follows:
the head and part of the neck, two pieces of the thorax of the same
size, plus two pieces of the hips and legs. Thus, the fried guinea-
pig is divided into five pieces.

Some women make a quick peanut sauce by using the liver, the
heart and the kidneys. When they do so, it is normal to fry the
entrails in a frying pan or in a separate casserole. The majority of
our female informants point out that fried guinea-pig is 'less hard
work than the roasted guinea-pig'.

Boiled Guinea-pig

There is no agreement about boiled guinea-pig. In Sharvan, for instance, the women we interviewed almost unanimously agreed that boiled guinea-pig is 'really bad, and slimy as jelly'. However, boiling is common. The meat is chopped into pieces before boiling, as described above. Salt, pepper and cumin are spread on the animal, which is then put into a casserole with a little water. Soup made from guinea-pig meat is also common. The meat is boiled with carrots and cabbage, and sometimes with peas and yucca. After nearly twenty minutes, people often add pasta or rice. The result, in the majority of cases, is a very thick soup. Many women told us that to take away the taste of 'fresh' guinea-pig (which results in a 'bitter' or acid taste) it is desirable to fry it in lard for a few minutes. In none of the variants of this dish was the importance of the dressings pointed out.

Guinea-pig stew constitutes one of the most common ways of cooking guinea-pig, together with roasting. Even if the main operation is boiling the meat, the process of cooking begins with frying pieces which have been well seasoned or, if there is more time, grilling them to the point at which the guinea-pig is 'half cooked' (this technique, though, is not used much or really well known). Then, the most common process is to boil the chopped guinea-pig together with peeled, medium-size potatoes. Before serving it, however, people cook it for a few minutes with a bit of milk, to which the broth is added. Coriander and oregano leaves are also added. In some houses, it is common to fry onion, cumin, garlic, salt and pepper in the pan before putting in the pieces of meat. In some communities, this stew is called guinea-pig broth.

It is important to remember that the term *locro* (stew) means a type of thick soup in Ecuador. In traditional highland cooking, various stews are the core of the meal or, better, 'food' *par excellence*. Soup is a 'starter'. Stew is a synthesis of various dishes, using lupin seeds, *chochos* (cinnamon seeds), potatoes, soft pumpkins, squashes or cheese. Stews are often served with avocado and chillies. They constitute a very rich culinary field, both semantically and practically, and are evidence of great cultural continuity in Ecuadorean cooking. This includes the famous *fanesca*, at Easter, a sort of stew with a thick sauce, which has many different rural and urban variants.

Without exaggeration, one might say that Ecuadorean stews represent cookery done with emotion; they are dishes done with good taste, with natural simplicity, utilizing meat and vegetables, and call for considerable technical skills, which are part of wider ideas about maintaining the heat of the body in a mountain climate in which there are often sudden changes of temperature. Therefore stews are used throughout the year, in all seasons, on all 'normal' occasions. Stews are domestic food, the food of 'endogenous' cooking, especially for the family. In this respect, the use of saucepans and prolonged boiling helps maintain calories and preserves combinations of taste which get lost in roasting guinea-pig meat. Stews take a long time to cook and, despite the search for novelty – characteristic of other traditional Ecuadorean specialities, such as *tamales*[14] – are products of peasant common sense, based on sharp tastes and solid textures.

We have also encountered three variants of stews: guinea-pig stew, *colada* guinea-pig and guinea-pig in sauce. When people cook it as a stew, they begin as if they were preparing a *locro*, but when the basic fried ingredients are put into the casserole a good quantity of tomatoes are then added. The mixture is then cooked at low heat with small whole potatoes. To prepare the *colada*, many different types of flour are used – normally barley or bean flour. At the end, finely chopped potatoes are added. The final result is a soup much thicker than *locro*, called a *colada*. Guinea-pig in sauce is prepared with pieces of meat cooked at a very low heat in a clay pot and covered with a lid, adding just a little water. The result is a golden and crispy guinea-pig, which is served together with boiled potatoes that have been cooked with plenty of chillies.

Baked Guinea-pig

Obviously baked guinea-pig calls for a proper bread oven, which can be found only in the houses of more prosperous mestizo peasants who make bread. The procedure is the same as that used in preparing roast guinea-pig. The animal is slaughtered a day ahead, is well seasoned and is then laid on the grill in the oven. Normally people use the hot oven just after they have baked bread. This means that both the bread-making and the slaughtering of guinea-pigs require planning. The dish is served with *mote*, potatoes and white rice. Many of our informants suggest that this way of cooking is nearly as good as roasting guinea-pig.

A Comparative Digression

Guinea-pigs are much used in Peruvian cuisine, in both mestizo and Indian cooking. In the wider context of traditional cuisine in the Andean region, Peruvian cuisine is famed for its complexity, creativity and openness to multiple influences. There are therefore many different traditional ways of cooking guinea-pig. Roasted and well-seasoned guinea-pig served with potatoes and chillies, for instance, is one set of variations on the central theme of fried guinea-pig. From an analysis of sixteen recipes, I found that only five were based on frying. In another five, frying was merely a final touch to a broth, made by boiling.[15] Broths are made from a base of fried onions and tomatoes and, in most cases, water, although refined mestizo cuisine uses wine and nuts as bases. The result, therefore, is more varied than in Ecuador. This can also be seen in the fact that the guinea-pig is baked and often roasted not only on charcoal but also on heated stones (*pachamanca*), and in many cases fried in one piece. When the frying is done quickly, the skinned guinea-pig is marinated in brine for one or two hours, and then allowed to thoroughly dry out. In order to fry an animal in one piece, the most commonly used technique is to place a very heavy stone on the top of the guinea-pig, which helps to keep it in a stretched position once it is put in the frying-pan. This technique is called *chatado*. The *chatado* guinea-pig is one of the most popular dishes in the restaurants of Arequipa and is often served with creole sauce, half-cooked potatoes and *mote*, or with hot chillies.[16]

Peruvian cooking is 'hotter' that Ecuadorean. In many recipes, the 'hot' component is important in providing both taste and colour. One of the traditional Indian dishes is known as *puku* (coloured) guinea-pig. Central to this dish is the cooking of meat which has been previously boiled in a sauce made with strongly coloured sunflower hot sauce, cumin, black pepper and annatto. Then, after lengthy cooking, during which the guinea-pig acquires a reddish brown colour from the combination of chillies, cumin and annatto, the meat is served with potatoes and fresh cheese. Variations in the spiciness of the meat depend on the type of chillies used: red, yellow or green, or combinations of different kinds. Roast guinea-pig is normally served with a hot sauce known as *uchullachua*, made with yellow and red chillies mixed with coriander and parsley, which are green and so create a yellowish green, very visually attractive dough. Crumbly cheese is added to this mixture. The roasted guinea-pigs are served with this sauce and with half-cooked potatoes.[17] Another common recipe in Peruvian cuisine is *pepian* of guinea-pig, which is made with cornflour added to the conventional frying base. Once this thick dough is made, the fried guinea-pigs are added, together with some roasted maize. This is usually served with parboiled potatoes or with *mote*.[18]

In mestizo cuisine, people use different types of alcohol to marinate the meat of the guinea-pig: strong *chicha* (maize liquor) or white or red wine. In Peru, the *secos* are dishes which, despite their name, are rich in broth and sauce. In some recipes, the guinea-pig is not only marinated in alcohol, but is also cooked in it. In all these cases, the guinea-pig is fried in advance or, in some dishes, may be added to the sauce, once the guinea-pig is sliced into pieces. We noted that white or red wine may be used in making the base of the *fricasé*[19] or guinea-pig stew. *Chicha* is only used as a marinade and not as a main ingredient in cooking.

In Peru – in clear contrast to Ecuador – various guinea-pig-based dishes are part of the ordinary menu of mestizo restaurants and taverns (bars). In most taverns and restaurants in middle-sized towns in the Ecuadorean sierra, it is possible to find only roast guinea-pig, and exceptionally, guinea-pig 'schnitzel'. Thus, rural peasant cooking in Ecuador is more varied than urban or semi-urban commercial cooking. On the other hand, in Peruvian cooking there is a certain degree of higher, urban 'legitimacy' and a higher level of experimentation, in which the use of alcohol in cooking and the search for variations of form, colour and taste seem to be important concerns.[20]

The world of guinea-pig cuisine is not limited to the analysis of recipes and techniques of food transformation. This symbolic world goes beyond the analysis of particular flavours intimately associated with culinary pleasure, and only acquires meaning if it is transformed within a social world that is shared by the actors. Hence one of the central issues is to determine when and how people eat different types of guinea-pig dishes. All cooking can be seen as a 'social calendar', where social actors become the main characters in a process of synthesis – through food – of ritual times and special places. This is what happens in our Ecuadorean communities.

Occasions, Events and Reasons for Eating Guinea-pig

Up to now we have analysed the guinea-pig's semantic logic through recipes. In this context of cultural creativity, combining guinea-pig meat with other ingredients entails transformations of meaning because of the different tastes and textures involved. In one way, cooking the guinea-pig allows its real transformation to take place. The death and slaughter of a guinea-pig makes possible not only the consumption of calories – in the sense used by Bolton and Calvin (1981) – but also the creative use of kitchen tools, greens, spices, vegetables, flour, alcohols and textures.

The function of the guinea-pig as 'cheap and nutritious' food, whether explicitly thought of by the actors involved or interpreted by observers, leads us now to wider issues of the relationship between symbols and social relations.

Although the axis of cultural mediation is central and involves a process of elaboration and reflection on the meaning of food, this does not preclude another important axis: the consumption and the social use of the guinea-pig.[21] In order to avoid cultural bias, it is important to analyse the guinea-pig not only via recipes but also in its relation to those who consume it. In this respect, food articulates different types of social relations and allows us to analyse what is eaten, in which context and with whom. In other words, we see society in movement. Food is not therefore a symbol in itself, a closed 'text' abstracted from social reality, but an act which is mainly social, an opening to the world that allows people to experience commensality and to symbolize different kinds of social relations, while still involving a material content.[22]

Thus, while eating, people both reproduce daily food routines and celebrate ritual occasions or social events that are important to the social actors. Likewise, food can be a pretext for the expression of consideration, greetings and one's interests in certain social ties – the fulfilment of a promise or a contract, or even generosity and hospitality. Occasions, events and pretexts have to be analysed in order to see whether guinea-pigs are an exceptional food. However, independently of observers, informants also attribute to the guinea-pigs a special value and special place in the system of local social status.

Only in Sharván did we encounter the notion that guinea-pigs can be consumed regularly and are not objects for special occasions of consumption – expressed in comments like 'We eat guinea-pig when we feel like it' or 'when we have run out of supplies of pasta and rice'. However, even in this community, guinea-pigs seem to be associated with festive and exceptional meals. In the other communities, the guinea-pig is an exceptional and 'structured' food. By 'structured' food, I mean not only that a sequence has to be followed, but also that there is an explicit association between recipes and occasions. We shall come back to this later in this chapter. Now we are going to examine links with the festival calendar.

Undoubtedly, the festival calendar is fundamental in the rural communities and villages of the Ecadorean sierra, the basic outline of which is as follows:

Magi (The Three Kings): 6 January
Carnival and Ash Wednesday: variable between the first week
    in February and the first week in March
Easter and Holy Week: between the second week of March and
    the second week of April
Corpus Christi, variable: between the last week of May and 2 June
Day of the Dead: 2 November
Christmas: 25 December
New Year: 31 December

Between Holy Week and Corpus Christi, harvest-time begins, early on at the end of April with the harvest of soft maize and ending with the harvest of hard maize at the end of June. In June everywhere in the sierra, San Pedro, San Pablo and San Juan are also celebrated. The calendar becomes denser at the time of weeding and earthing up in November and December.[23] All these celebrations require the presence of the guinea-pig. In addition, offices, such as that of *prioste*, entail a system of social relations based on services and counter-services, in which food and drink are important components in the celebrations. In most public meals where food is widely available, such as Carnival, Holy Week, Corpus Christi, All Saints or special communal celebrations, guinea-pig meat has less importance than roast beef and pork. However, on those days or on special days within the busy calendar of these celebrations – what we might call 'days of thanksgiving' – guinea-pigs are also offered to a priest, to a political official or to a godfather or godmother, especially on Easter Sunday and the Saturday before Lent.

Many of the religious celebrations are celebrated at a more local level. In Guzo, Santa Rosa, at the end of August, is usually a festive day. The feast of San Francisco, on the 4 October, is also celebrated in Guzo and in Llactahurco and Chirinche. In Llactahurco, San Antonio is usually celebrated in June and the Virgin of Tránsito in August. The religious calendar in Tigualó is relatively packed: Santa Marianita in the month of September, San Vicente in April, and San Isidro on 24 May. However, these celebrations are not very 'communal' nowadays, rather occasions for family gatherings. In Tigualó, for instance, the only celebration communally carried out is the festival of the 'captains' at the end of the year. This cannot take place without the economic assistance and the direct participation of young migrants, who return to the community during that period. However, in some cases guinea-pig will be eaten 'as it should be' in all the celebrations which are organized around specific saints and rituals of the Virgin which have local or national relevance. These feasts, not being 'compulsory', are certainly not celebrated with any intention simply of consuming protein.

The possibility of determining the 'character' of a festival has increased with the increase of migration and of seasonal geographical mobility among the Ecuadorean peasantry. This can be seen by looking at festivals that have a more 'national' character. In less-organized celebrations, at community level and with a family character, such as the Three Kings, Christmas and New Year, guinea-pig is the favourite dish and people always choose to serve it roasted. In all these celebrations, the number of guinea-pigs never exceeds one guinea-pig for each adult man, half a guinea-pig for women and youths, and three or four portions for the youngsters, regardless of their sex. In this way, the number of guinea-pigs that are slaughtered for each feast cannot, on these occasions, exceed one and a half dozen. Relatives and close godparents are invited for Boxing Day or New Year's Day.

In some Indian communities, such as Palmira Dávalos, the tradition of the 'Kings' still exists. This consists in making a 'castle' – nothing more than a little shed – in which roasted guinea-pigs are hung as offerings to the Kings, who will come to visit the community. Normally two people are in charge of this ceremony: one builds the palace and the other plays the role of one of the 'Three Magi'. They are in charge of distributing the hanged guinea-pigs among participants. It is interesting to remember that the tradition of the 'castle' of Corpus Christi; – which is found in highland communities – has no direct link with 'palaces', though. 'Castles' are large boards that are placed on a pole at a certain height, on which prizes are positioned which have to be reached by climbing the greasy pole. On this castle, there are often prizes such as live guinea-pigs, birds, bags filled with corn-cobs, bottles of drink and plastic objects.

The religious calendar functions as a sort of framework that marks out and delimits the ritual occasions on which guinea-pigs are consumed. Productive strategies have to meet these require-ments. Obviously it is not possible to totally plan this production cycle, since some families will not have enough guinea-pigs available by the dates on which they ought to offer them to relatives, authorities and godparents. The fact than any adult is immersed in a circuit of social relations involves not only offering guinea-pigs but also making returns for those consumed on earlier occasions. In the wider system of Andean reciprocity – which includes at least two annual festive cycles – the roles of provider and consumer are interchangeable. According to female informants, the continuous production of guinea-pigs allows people to participate in a system of social relations involving offerings; religious celebrations follow a more repetitive and broader time context. It is women who have to plan the production of guinea-pigs, so that men and the other members of their family can participate in the ritual interchange of food. As against Bolton and Calvin (1981), the central require-ment is that of taking part in a system of reciprocity and ritual exchange, rather than the mere consumption of protein at times of maximum shortage.[24] When a man in the extended family has an important ritual duty, such as *prioste*, the rest of his family will help him to assemble the considerable number of animals needed for the slaughter. In mestizo communities, in particular, it is believed that if guinea-pigs are not offered on religious occasions 'God will punish us'.

In the celebrations we have mentioned, regulated by a strict religious calendar, guinea-pig and other food make it possible for families to participate in public life, on some occasions as consumers, on others as those providing the offerings. The same elements inform celebrations offered for patrons of the com-munity. The spread of cults of the saints and the Virgin in the Andes, for instance, took place relatively far away from residential centres.[25] This implies that such cults involve pilgrimages to certain sepulchres, such as that of the Virgin of Agua Santa in Baños or the Virgin of Quinche, near Quito. To carry out these pilgrimages – which can last up to several days – many of our female informants point out that people need to take with them 'festive food' – roasted guinea-pig served cold, together with cooked beans, *mote*, roasted maize and cooked potatoes.

However, religious cults of the saints and the Virgins[26] can also be private, since in some communities there are families which are very devoted to their saints and to the Virgin. Images of saints and of the Virgins are kept in small altars in the house, and feasts, and, when possible, masses (though rare), are organized in their honour. Hence a family needs to provide food for those present at these ceremonies. The guinea-pig is again central. In many cases up to twenty to thirty animals may be slaughtered. Obviously, the system of exchange to which I have previously referred makes it possible to carry out, if necessary, the *jocha* – a contribution of animals – by the close family, strengthening the network of exchange in local and regional religious contexts.

Women play the main role as 'producers' of food in community, local and regional religious contexts. Even if men hold most public positions of prestige and central roles in these festivals, the symbolic articulation between ceremony, religious ritual and food is predominantly a female 'function'. Likewise, at the domestic level, the cult of the 'family's' saints and of the Virgin is mainly an activity to which women are more 'devoted' than men.

Juxtaposed to the religious calendar is the farming calendar. This superimposition creates occasions for another kind of special consumption of guinea-pigs. We found a clear relation between tasks associated with the cultivation of maize and the consumption of guinea-pigs. In this reproductive context, the guinea-pig appears to reinforce 'mutual aid' at times when extra labour is required: sowing, weeding, earthing up and harvesting. This system of exchange does not call for an additional supply of food because work is paid with work. But providing guinea-pig meat – possibly roasted – is something 'additional', a manifestation of appreciation, which strengthens social obligations. In mestizo communities, a common idea is that when a person has been given a guinea-pig, he/she will feel obliged to make a return by doing reciprocal work. But when cultivating potatoes – a type of cultivation which is more commercial, like that of maize – monetary payment is an important form of reward, as well as the provision of reciprocal labour.

In the presence of pure 'wage relations', we never found any additional offering of food. Where rewards are mixed – wages plus food – guinea-pigs are not part of the edibles used. In some cases, especially in mestizo communities, having guinea-pigs to offer as a form of mutual aid is seen to be a 'good investment', since in this way 'money is saved'. Not possessing guinea-pigs is perceived as a situation of extreme shortage, since it is a standardized and expected part of this kind of labour exchange and a ritual endorsement of social relations generally.

In Ayanquil, a very typical traditional mestizo community, sharecropping relations are very common. The most common offering, after the harvest, is to give the owner of the land a couple of 'well-roasted' guinea-pigs. This ceremony expresses not only appreciation, but also an interest in renewing the contract for the following season. The act of accepting the guinea-pigs that are offered is considered to be a positive sign that the land will again be granted in the following year to the person offering the gift. Some of our informants emphasized the fact that more guinea-pigs 'given away' – when people increase the gift from a few to a greater number – may indicate that they have an interest in renting more land. Likewise, once a lot of land has been obtained, people offer more than the standard couple of guinea-pigs as a sign of their deep appreciation. The same logic exists in the case of the loan of a team of oxen: these are returned with a couple of roast guinea-pigs.

The guinea-pig, then, is associated with a set of social relations of a more profane character, where the main concern is ensuring the acquisition of crucial resources needed for the reproductive cycle: labour and land. In this context, the guinea-pig is a social articulator, which reinforces reciprocity, and a concrete material reward into the bargain. Undoubtedly, the fact that guinea-pigs are offered as food is seen by the participants as a sign of the importance that is assigned to these kinds of social relations. When our informants talk about 'social possibilities' at this level, they refer to the fact of having guinea-pigs ready to be offered. Possessing money allows people to employ labour in the market; having guinea-pigs allows them to establish and reproduce social relations.

The initiation and reproduction of privileged links with particular people is thus definitely marked by the offering of guinea-pigs. We have seen above that after every important celebration guinea-pigs are offered to local and regional political authorities, thereby recognizing a system of public status that is based on the symbolic and real power of the offices and the authority, not the character or competence of the actual people who hold offices. The 'establishment' of social relations is an activity that nobody and no community can escape from. People are born into a family, with a 'genealogy', and into a community. Both can be seen as a kind of 'accident' or as 'destiny', depending on your point of view. However, in order to become 'persons', over a certain period of time, they need to be part of a ceremonial and ritual system, whose central core consists of established social relations and the establishing of new ones. One of the most important of these, in Ecuador, is to ask somebody to stand as godparent to children who are due to be baptized, confirmed or wed. These visits, arranged in advance by women, are always accompanied by presents, which consist of a couple of roasted guinea-pigs. The same happens when the hand of the fiancée, or of the woman who has been chosen by the son, is 'asked' for in marriage: on these occasions, fathers also have to offer a few well-roasted guinea-pigs, if possible straight from the grill. After the father of the fiancée has agreed to 'hand her over', the groom normally pays a visit soon afterwards and is expected not to turn up with empty hands. For our female informants, the ideal is to arrive with many guinea-pigs for the parents of the future spouse and a few for the fiancée. The engaged woman can dispose of her guinea-pigs as she wishes. In such cases, it is assumed that the guinea-pigs will be roasted.

As we might expect, these ceremonies are preludes to fiestas: the traditional celebrations of baptism, first communion and weddings. A wedding is celebrated with a big feast, where – if possible – plenty of food and drink is offered. Guinea-pigs are also provided. When the time for these celebrations draws near, it is advisable, if possible, to 'save up' a great quantity of guinea-pigs.

When people take part in a funeral, especially in Indian communities, it is customary to offer a few guinea-pigs to the relatives of the dead person. The family of the deceased person has to take charge of preparing enough food and drink for those who participate in the wake and the burial.

In the examples I have mentioned, we can see the way in which a family, and many of its members, who occupy different roles which change over time, are involved in a sequence of ceremonies in which the domestic development cycle and the religious and farming calendars influence the type of events and the food provided. The guinea-pig is at the centre, but it is not the only animal, since beef, lamb or pork is also part of these meals. However, most of these types of meat, even if highly regarded (especially pork), do not have the same significance as guinea-pig meat in the overall system of ritual values. It is the guinea-pig that has the most prominent role in the articulation of status and occasion, of positions and power, of services and rewards. It is a special component in the pragmatic and symbolic world of these communities.

Regardless of the special character of the guinea-pig as food, there are other unplanned accessories which justify its death and consequent consumption. These occasions are less ritualized than those we have discussed and are used to show appreciation on occasion of an unexpected visit by a child, a godparent, a cherished relative or an important person. When this happens, an animal is normally slaughtered and then offered to the visitor while the family eats conventional food. The guinea-pig thus marks the 'exceptionality' of the person and, even more so, the 'exceptionality' of the occasion. In our previous examples, we have seen how special occasions and events call for the consumption of guinea-pig: the 'structured consumption' of the animal is an intrinsic part of the social situation being celebrated. A guinea-pig can become a 'pretext' when an event is unexpected, an important occasion which cannot be planned because there is no fixed date or occasion in the minds of the particular actors who are making the offering. In this way, an unexpected, yet 'cherished' and 'treasured', visitor receives a real and definite tribute.

Parallel with this kind of 'structured consumption', Sunday consumption is also found, though less frequently. This type of consumption depends on the quantity of guinea-pig which people have available and on the cycle of family festivals for the following months. In many mestizo communities, the importance of eating meat is emphasized, even if it is not eaten more than once a week. This meat is usually bought, since a 'big' animal cannot be slaughtered for the consumption of just one family. Therefore, people think it better to slaughter a few guinea-pigs to make a *colada* or a 'fry-up'. These usages show that the ideology of the guinea-pig as an exceptional food is still dominant in the Ecuadorean sierra. The indications are that this will still be the case for a long time to come.

Conclusion: Culinary Logic and Social Logic

Cooking guinea-pigs in special ways involves a set of 'secrets' which are culinary in themselves but are also affected by wider social considerations. Obviously, a system of tastes, flavours and colours can only be understood when it is put into operation. We have seen this in the case of the guinea-pig, which is transformed into 'dishes', in relation to events and to what we have called 'pretexts'. Without doubt, roast guinea-pig constitutes the highest point of the pyramid of culinary prestige in Ecuador. It is as if the peasant world – following the metaphoric description of Lévi-Strauss – is converted into an aristocratic one at the moment of celebration. Therefore roast guinea-pig is provided on all important, religious feast-days as well as in the ceremonies that mark important family occasions. The act of serving a whole roast guinea-pig is considered to be a major privilege, exclusively reserved for adult men. Fried guinea-pig also has a certain prestige, both culinarily and socially. Boiled guinea-pig, though, is not a festive food.[27]

Thus, the guinea-pig is central in Indian culinary traditions, and over time has become consolidated in a rural tradition that oversteps ethnic boundaries. The guinea-pig is not just the hottest and most tasty kind of meat, but the one that creates important differences: it differentiates occasions of structured and exceptional consumption from less structured, everyday consumption. Ecuadorean diet has undergone a series of transformations in recent years, as a result of the 'modernization' of styles of consumption. The consumption of rice and pasta has increased in both Indian and mestizo populations, and the consumption of locally produced flour made from maize, beans, barley and peas has decreased. However, potatoes remain an important element in the diet and are still eaten in their traditional forms as *locro* soup or as a *colada*. A typical day for 'traditional' food in the sierra is composed of breakfast – a *colada* of wheat, barley, oats, peas, beans or potatoes, especially at the time of harvest; a hot dish prepared for people when they come back from work at dusk, consisting of a *locro* of potatoes, beans and cabbage; and, in the evening – if there is enough – a *colada* of beans, flour and potatoes. If people are a long way from home, their diet, during the working day, normally consists of beans and unpeeled potatoes. Soups or *coladas* can be transformed by using sugar, salt or 'very little' salt. Generally speaking, the morning soup is sweet, that at lunchtime never so, while the evening meal can be any of the three types. The increasing use of rice and pasta in today's diet threatens the traditional role of many different kinds of flour made from potatoes and pulses. Given this dietary context, the shortage of animal protein, as well as of vitamins, is obvious. Consumption of vegetables and fruit is restricted to festive days. Because of these considerations, some commentators have tended to treat rural Ecuadoreans as being particularly concerned with protein deficiency and to see the guinea-pig as a possible solution to this problem.

I have shown that the guinea-pig is important and is eaten throughout the whole year. To the six major traditional celebrations (seven, if we include celebration of patron saints), we would have to add five or six occasions on top of these during a 'normal' yearly cycle for the family. Guinea-pigs, then, are consumed at least once a month. If we think in terms of traditional standard quantities this is not much, and is less so for children, who, for various reasons, need more protein. Guinea-pig – like other meat eaten in Ecuador – is not part of the daily diet, not even the 'Sunday meal'.

In the following chapter, we shall examine another form of consumption altogether, which is not related to celebrations or commemorations of important occasions in family and community life, but to the traditional health-care system. The guinea-pig is here transformed from a ritual and festive food into a healing food.

Notes

1. See especially Mintz (1985). Mintz shows impressively the importance of sugar in the modernization process in European countries, especially its changing importance in nutrition and as a major source of flavour. Sugar and, to a certain extent, 'sweet' things, once luxuries of the upper classes and the European aristocracy, have become an essential part of working-class diet. In the Ecuadorean peasant diet and the diet of the poorest urban groups, the amount of calories eaten in the form of the use and abuse of sucrose is indisputably one of the problems associated with inadequate diet. None the less, this does not negate the importance of 'sweet' things as foods that give a great deal of pleasure. We might even extend this to the kind of alcoholic drinks that people enjoy: *chicha* and rum are undoubtedly very sugary.

2. In many communities, our informants tend to agree that the 'hottest' meat used to be wild deer, which was more available in the past. Today, however, these deer have practically disappeared in the sierra.
3. There is general agreement that fish is the coldest meat. Fish, however, is part of a wider classificatory system, since what it is compared with are 'earthy' meats.
4. See particularly Luna de la Fuente and Moreno Rojas (1969, p. 89), who demonstrate the 'quality' of guinea-pig, as compared with other meat, via a percentage analysis of its chemical composition:

	Water	Protein	Fat	Minerals
Guinea-pig	70.6	20.3	7.8	0.8
Fowl	70.2	18.5	9.3	1.0
Pork	46.8	14.5	37.3	0.7
Lamb	50.6	16.4	31.1	1.0
Beef	58.9	17.5	21.8	1.0

These authors argue that the rapid growth of a litter depends on the quality of the milk, which is very rich in albuminoids (proteins); guinea-pig milk contains 11.9% albuminoids as against 3.8% in cows' milk. The fat ratio is 45.8% in the case of guinea-pig milk as against 3.7% for cows' milk. This is to say that guinea-pig milk is very 'concentrated, which makes possible an extraordinarily rapid development of this species' (1978, p. 44).

5. The same type of slaughter has been observed by Bolton and Calvin in Peru (1981, pp. 290–1). Even though they did not observe this technique in the communities they studied, they point out that the technique of breaking the neck bones of the animal through wrenching is common. We did not actually find this method in Ecuador. Bolton and Calvin point out that this does not seem to be the 'ideal' form since it allows blood to be absorbed into the meat. This practice may seem horrific to those people who are not used to any type of slaughter. Michelle O. Fried writes in her excellent book on traditional Ecuadorean recipes:

> I would have wished to describe the way guinea-pigs are slaughtered, but when I heard the neck bones breaking I had to give it up. The noise haunted me for a whole day. Since then I have not touched a live guinea-pig. None the less, I have to admit that I much enjoy a well-cooked one. (1986, p. 91)

6. The entrails are normally eaten, but not in any kind of dish. We shall come back to this point later in this chapter when I present some of the most common recipes.

7. Leach writes:

> When we look into the facts, the categories which are treated as significant *kinds* of food become interesting in themselves. The diet of any particular human population is dependent upon the availability of resources and, at the level of actual items of foodstuff (bread, mutton, cheese and so on), there is very little overlap between the shopping list of an English housewife and the Amazonian Indian. But the English housewife and the Amazonian Indian alike break up the unitary category 'food' into a number of subcategories, 'food A', 'food B', 'food C', etc., each of which is treated in a different way. (1970, p. 32) (Leach's italics).

Sahlins (1976) has rightly remarked that in modern and complex societies the symbolic construction of what can be eaten matches the productive scheme, by matching supply and demand, resulting in a 'global totemic order', which brings together, in a sort of parallel differences, the status of those who eat and the status of what they eat. This idea is undoubtedly valid for other contexts in which the meat culture of North American society is absent. We shall examine this when discussing ways of eating guinea-pig in rural Ecuador, where the establishment of particular social differences is also central.

8. For a systematic discussion of the culinary triangle in Lévi-Strauss see, among others, Leach (1970, pp. 29–35) and Goody (1982, pp. 17–29). Lehrer (1969, 1972) has illustrated, in a very useful way, the advantages and disadvantages of the structuralist approach. Lehrer writes:

> Lévi-Strauss is correct, I believe, in arguing that it is possible to say something about cooking in general without respect to any particular culture. Moreover, it is possible to establish a relatively small set of components that will describe the opposition of cooking terms in all languages (though each language will not use them all). The components cannot all be binary, like phonological distinctive features. Lévi-Strauss' main error, however, is to assume that we can have a neutral structure of cooking concepts that will be valid for all languages. (1972, p. 169).

9. For the analysis of Lévi-Strauss, see especially Lévi-Strauss (1965, pp. 19–20, 1968, pp. 390–411). The 'simple' culinary triangle of Lévi-Strauss has the following form:

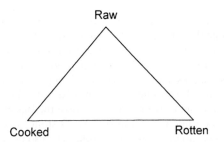

From the raw to the cooked, the transformative operation is mainly cultural, while the transformation into the rotten is natural. A more comprehensive triangle can be obtained from this one by combining it with the main techniques of food transformation:

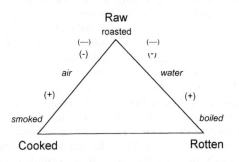

10. Lévi-Strauss writes:

> What, then, constitutes the opposition between the roast and the boiled? Roasted food, being directly exposed to fire, is in a relationship of *non-mediatized conjunction*, whereas boiled food is the product of a twofold process of mediation: it is immersed in water and both food and water are contained within a receptacle. (1968, p. 397)

11. Lévi-Strauss observes on this subject that:

> boiling provides a method of preserving all the meat and its juices, whereas roasting involves destruction or loss. One suggests economy, the other waste; the second is aristocratic, the first plebeian. (1968, p. 401)

12. Lévi-Strauss, after having introduced his enlarged model – where the central point is still the roasted, the smoked and the boiled – argues strongly that it is not possible to imagine that all culinary systems follow this model (1968, pp. 406–11), which is therefore only

one system of possible transformations. He comments that it is conceivable that, if there were no technique of smoking, there would be other ways of preserving food, as for instance drying meat in the open air without salt (and, one might add, in the sun with no salt). These techniques, naturally become changed once salt is added. On the other hand, complications can arise with the use of different tools. Lévi-Strauss – using the example of the Blackfoot – shows that food can be boiled in ceramic pots, in stone vessels, in very soft leather bags and in wooden casseroles. He also uses the term 'roast' to cover two techniques: 'roasting' and 'grilling' (1968, pp. 409–10). In the case of grilling, meat is placed very close to the fire. Therefore, roasting is midway between grilling and smoking. Finally, he acknowledges that a more complete transformation takes place with the introduction of frying. Frying implies the supply of an important element, together with fire and water: oil or other types of animal or vegetable fat. Therefore, additional techniques have to be added to the original axis of transformation, which imply a process of drying, the use of a grill and, finally, the act of frying. This model is thus more complex. These observations do not exhaust the possibilities of different techniques of food-transformation found in complex culinary practices. We could make the model even more complex if we added the origin (vegetable or animal) and the kind of food used, as well as taking into account techniques for producing a particular kind of food. These few lines are enough to remind us that a search for a comparative, simple formula in the thinking of Lévi-Strauss does not capture the complexities found in the analysis of concrete cases. Lévi-Strauss is always trying to shape his analysis in such a way as to highlight continuities and repetitions in the search for cultural universals. This implies accepting, at the same time, that the specific content of cultural practices is very varied. It may seem almost banal to point this out, but maybe this does not happen by chance as it is often thought.

13. *Cebiche* is raw fish marinated in lemon juice [translator's note].

14. *Tamales* are minced meat and maize dough, normally wrapped in a maize husk [translator's note].

15. My analysis is fundamentally based on recipes included in the book *Biblioteca Agropecuaria* (Anon., 1978, pp. 157–76). This book was published as a part of a nationalist policy aiming at replacing the consumption of beef by increasing the consumption of 'national' meat: fish and guinea-pig. The recipes – eighteen in all – sum up existing popular culinary traditions and are consequently a good summary of Peruvian cuisine. The author or authors of the book (anonymous, as is the case with many popular books of a technical character published in various countries of Latin America) deliberately emphasize the importance of the decision of the Peruvian

government to go for the commercial production of guinea-pigs on a big scale in order to solve national food problems. The book is intended to be a manual for rural development workers. The modern techniques suggested, which imply breeding guinea-pigs outside the home, are illustrated by an excellent presentation of traditional cooking, in the context of the symbolic value of the animal for health and the prevention of diseases. Nowhere, though, do the author/ authors envisage that there is any relationship between the type of breeding and the way the animal is used. The impact of modernization, therefore, is not taken into account.

16. This analysis of Peruvian cooking is limited in two aspects: I did not carry out a systematic analysis of the dozen books available on typical Peruvian cuisine, nor have I done fieldwork in Peru. My contacts with the practice of guinea-pig cooking are limited to visiting restaurants in Arequipa many years ago, and are therefore fading memories.

17. The preparation of this dressing is a particularly sought-after aesthetic experience. Combining different types of chillies, the objective is to achieve the production of a 'greenish dough with an appealing and artistic look'.

18. We read that:

> *Pepian* is a Peruvianism which indicates the name of a dish made with grated soft maize and chillies, and normally cooked with meat (pork, fowl, guinea-pig) or fresh cheese. *Pepian* seems to derive from *pepa*, a widely used Americanism which indicates *pepita*, 'seed (or stone) of fruit'. Then, the origin of *pepian* might be a mixture made with pumpkin seeds and chillies. (Anon., 1978, pp. 162–3)

19. *Fricasé* is a dish prepared with meat already cooked that is then refried with lard [translator's note].

20. In the culinary, urban and ideological world of Ecuador, the 'death' of the guinea-pig is obvious. The guinea-pig becomes a peasant, rural and also typically Indian dish. We did not find any recipe for guinea-pig in the two most popular recipe books of the sierra: LERT (1982), reprinted four times in two years, and Ordóñez de Cobos (1984), reprinted fifteen times up to this year. However, in books that profess to be about 'traditional' cooking, and which are so, to a certain extent – Doña Juanita (1986, pp. 201–2) and Michelle O. Fried (1986, pp. 88–9) – guinea-pig, as a traditional dish, is always presented as 'roast guinea-pig'. Both books are actually valuable – the second being the more systematic – and give us some idea of the richness of Ecuadorean 'traditional, popular' cuisine, in which there is a mixture of different influences – regional and associated with different rural and urban classes. Obviously the cooking of guinea-pig is not limited

to Peru and Ecuador. Nelly de Jordan (1979, pp. 221–6) writes about
three recipes from Bolivia, one of soup and two of fried guinea-pig,
while Castaño Quintero (1979, pp. 44–6) presents five traditional
recipes from the province of Nariño, Colombia – the only place
where guinea-pigs are actually bred. These recipes are similar to
traditional recipes in other Andean countries: roast as well as boiled,
cooked or half-cooked guinea-pig. The theme of the two recipe
books – defined as 'traditional' or 'modern' as a part of an attempt
to create a 'national cuisine' – needs greater detailed analysis. These
questions become important when we observe the attempt to
formulate 'national' identities on the base of well-established
'regional' styles of cooking (see especially Appadurai, 1988).

21. In an analysis of food, Lange (1975) discerns a different axis in the
transformation of perishable elements. Firstly, he distinguishes an
axis of immersion in the world in relation to the origin of food
elements; secondly, an axis of maturation – which concerns the study
of processes of transformation of raw food; and, thirdly, an axis of
intervention, which consists in bringing order into the world and
'appropriating' it. At this level, culinary practices and the social
world of meals stress discontinuities as between society and the
natural world and between things of the world, since a hierarchy of
objects to be consumed and of objects to be transformed is
established. Last is the axis of learning – understanding the social
world through the meaning of food. To a certain extent, my analysis
of consumption and social use is a combination of the last two axes
of this analysis.

22. If we limit ourselves to the idea that food 'symbolizes' social relations,
we cannot escape from what we might call the 'Durkheimian trap':
that food 'expresses' a specific social structure. This idea is central
to a great part of modern anthropology, functionalist and structuralist alike. In this focus, the emphasis is therefore upon the unity
of culture, on 'cultural order', without recognizing the possibility
of internal variations. We need, however, to take into account
external influences, and the relevance of history, as well as the effect
of material elements that are not under our control. My analysis tries
to examine sociocultural variations and the 'meeting' of two different sociocultural logics – on the one hand, the modern logic of
technical specialists and experts and, on the other, a rural 'logic'.

23. Rueda has observed that: 'The celebrations that peasants adopt most
often are those linked to the agricultural cycle, some with pre-
Colombian roots' (1982, p. 171).

24. As I have mentioned, Bolton and Calvin (1981) emphasize that the
ritual cycle is a 'pretext' for consuming guinea-pigs, but that, in
reality, the underlying issue is the shortage of protein. Yet we shall

see that this deficit is not solved by ritual consumption. Therefore, the aspects that I have stressed in pointing to a wider system of interchange seem central to me. The interesting point is that Bolton and Calvin – sophisticated observers as they are – follow closely the different social contexts in which the guinea-pig appears. In other words, not only the fiesta but also the status of the individual is important. When one is a godfather or *compadre*, the chances of eating guinea-pig increase and, at the same time, cumulate, since people enter into a system of social relations. Over time, a godfather/*compadre* will need other godfathers/*compadres*.

25. On this point see particularly Sallnow (1991).
26. Although, of course, there is only one mother of Christ, she is worshipped at different places where she is believed to have appeared, e.g. the Virgin of Guadalupe.
27. We shall return to other aspects of food and the curative aspects of the guinea-pig in more detail in the next chapter.

CHAPTER FIVE

The Healing Meat

In previous chapters we examined guinea-pig meat from the point of view of its transformation into food, which is served at the feasts that mark every kind of special event in both individual and community life. In these cultural contexts, guinea-pigs as food are always forms of special and highly structured consumption. The intrinsic properties of hot and tasty guinea-pig meat, and its corresponding symbolic and social value, make for a greatly varied cuisine, with a marked degree of sophistication. Ecuadorean peasant culture – with its mestizo and Indian components – also includes guinea-pig meat within a field of cultural practices where it is possible to see an interplay between the hot and the cold and between cooking and health. This is inevitable, since food and cooking belong to a complex cultural sphere, in which the reproduction of the body, as part of a wider framework of reference, is fundamental both in social practice and in its cultural meanings.

Culinary practices are therefore related to ideas about health, since – as mentioned above – the majority of civilizations with long written traditions as well as many civilizations that have strong oral traditions share the belief that there are certain types of food which heat up the body – or part of it – and others which make it cooler or which are neutral. Generally speaking, this conception can be summarized according to the following principles:

1. The human body contains certain 'humours', 'qualities' or 'airs' which, since they are immaterial essences, control particular physiological processes.
2. These humours, traditionally, are the cold and the hot, the humid and the dry. In many accounts, the last two humours are unusual or play a minor role.

3. Health is maintained through a correct balance between different humours.
4. In some beliefs, specific types of combinations are associated with specific kinds of personality characteristics.
5. Elements external to the body can heat, cool, humidify or dry it: sun and warmth heat the body; water refreshes it. The majority of foods – like medicines – have these properties, the precise effects of which vary from culture to culture. However, empirical studies in different societies show that there are disagreements – in some case fundamental ones – between informants who classify meals and food in an exact way, rather than in general terms.[1]

This medical system, based on a theory of humours, has not only been found in very different cultural areas – such as Latin America, Europe and Asia – but has also been very persistent over time. As a 'popular' model it is still widely used, although advocates of modern, scientific models argue that it is incomplete and deficient, especially in relation to representations of the body and physiological processes. Let us summarize these.

The efficacy of these humoral models derives from many factors, firstly, because of their classificatory simplicity and, in many cultures, their precision;[2] secondly, as in the case of Bali, where all diseases can be classified as being either hot or cold, because of their range. Thirdly, this is due to the direct connection between the cause, the type of illness and the appropriate therapy. These therapies, besides providing quick and cheap treatment, suit the natural environment and the peasant economy. Fourthly, their efficacy derives from their capacity to engender ideal norms of behaviour which avoid excess and thus generate a feeling of responsibility, since 'having good health involves keeping the body at a balanced temperature at all times'. Fifthly, their efficacy derives from their practical significance in linking the human body to specific ways of perceiving natural elements and to seasonal and daily variations. Sixthly, it derives from its 'democratic' spread, because in urban environments, and not only in low-income ones, this type of knowledge is used fairly systematically in parallel with knowledge and practices that derive from modern medicine.

All these criteria apply to the Ecuadorean case. We need, though, to clarify certain ideas about guinea-pigs before turning to our empirical findings. At this point, the eager reader will be expecting a 'complete' presentation of all foods that have therapeutic properties. In Ecuador not all diseases can be reduced to cold and hot, even if in many cases dietary therapies advise colder or hotter food. Muñoz Bernand (1986), for instance, shows that in Ecuador the standard and accepted classification of illnesses into illnesses 'of God' and illnesses 'of the land' does not include all diseases, and that in consequence there is some confusion among experts on the subject. Following Foster's arguments, there are two systems of explanation – the 'personalistic', where illness is the result of the specific intervention of a human, animal, natural or supernatural agent, and the 'naturalistic', where illness is explained in terms of an interpersonal model and where there is appropriate ground for applying a humoral theory.[3] However, his ethnographic materials and those of other writers show that both systems coexist and that the sick person and his or her relatives can shift from one system to another without being worried about maintaining clear and precise logical boundaries. Thus the classification found in Pujilí by Muñoz Bernand (1986, pp. 196–8) allows him to distinguish various systems of 'pure' interpretation of illnesses: diseases 'of the land', 'of God', *desmando* (lack of control) and 'bad illness'. Among these four, only the *desmando* fits into the explanatory model of the theory of humours and the cold/hot opposition. This means that models of interpretation are varied and complex and that the humoral theory covers only a limited part of cultural practices connected with illness.[4] We shall examine this in greater detail later.

Desmando illnesses include colds, menstrual distress and illnesses involving 'emotion'. A sick person is usually a 'generic individual', a peasant (it is interesting to note that illnesses 'of the land' affect only 'Indians' – also spoken of as 'natives' (*naturales*)). Hence, the 'wider spectrum' of this theory relates to a cultural world that includes both Indians and mestizos, and both the rural and the urban world. The aetiology is clear: it is related to thermic action, to the consumption of opposing kinds of food and to emotional excess. Pathological conditions are due therefore to the infringement of anatomical, physiological and psychological norms, which helps set off a process of rupture of the organic and humoral equilibrium. The treatment of these sicknesses is the field of the traditional healer or of a 'practical' person – a person who has relevant abilities or experience in the family and community. The treatment consists of traditional herbal remedies, combining hot and cold plants with massages, decoctions and baths.[5] With good insight, Muñoz Bernand points out that the Indian conception of illness involves a moral element – the necessity of maintaining personal equilibrium and, conversely, the danger of losing control. In this logic, the idea of a force that can get out of control is central. Disease tends to free this force, which is contained in humours, blood, feelings and emotions.

At the same time, the theory of the cold and the hot helps to conceptualize the dangers that exist in the environment and therefore need to be avoided. 'Losing control' is not only an individual act, since, for that to happen, there must be some external cause. I have referred to the importance of maintaining the thermic equilibrium of the body and to the idea that sudden changes tend to produce general disturbances and, consequently, colds, bronchitis and lung ailments. It is important to point out that in traditional knowledge, passing from a hot to a cold state places the body in jeopardy and that getting cold is worse than getting hot. This reflects the general idea that the body is more sensitive to cold than to heat. Likewise, it is thought that the effect of cold is sudden while the effect of heat takes longer to show itself. Thus, in the sierra it is common, in both Indian and mestizo communities, to try and heat the body and to avoid cooling it when it is too hot. This implies that the effect of cold on a heated body will be both efficacious and rapid in restoring the lost equilibrium. When the body is cold, the effect of heat will take longer to work; consequently, more heat and a longer span of time are needed to produce the results sought for. This observation suggests a certain asymmetry in the concept: treatments and therapies based on heat – which include food – will take time to take effect and therefore to result in cure. We should not forget, though, that a heated body exposed to more heat gets into a vulnerable state: consequently, the danger does not derive from cold but from an over-lengthy exposure to heat.

This reasoning clearly indicates a code of behaviour in which thermic extremes of environment can and should be avoided. People must take precautions against rain or against exposing themselves to either humidity and water for too long or to strong sun, without taking suitable precautions. However, in the sierra everybody knows that the rainy season is associated with lung diseases, while it is more likely that during dry periods 'temperature' and undefined discomforts will appear. None the less, the relationship between the body, its temperature and the time of the day is central. In the morning, the body wakes up cold, and it takes a great part of the day to warm it up. The idea is that when the body heats up from the effect of work, sun and two meals – breakfast and lunch – the temperature of the environment begins to decrease. Dusk, which is sudden in Ecuador, since sunset is quick, coincides with a considerable decrease in temperature. At that time of day, the body is still warm and can therefore be affected by cold, which becomes more intense as night falls. The worst perils are between dusk and evening, a time of day in which peasants avoid exposing their bodies to the extremes of a harsh environment. This caution is seriously observed and shows that cold is the 'enemy', the major 'force' which people are concerned about and against which they consequently defend themselves. A paradoxical aspect is the definition of cold as something 'exceptional' or 'abnormal', even though it is actually the most common daily experience in the whole of the Ecuadorean sierra. Therefore prevention plays a leading role in personal conduct and in norms of rural behaviour.[6]

In sum, the logic of the cold and the hot belongs to the field of humoral theory, and in the Ecuadorean context is a cultural referent found both in the Indian and in the mestizo world. There is therefore a set of illnesses which have special aetiologies, treatments and therapies. In previous chapters, we saw the implications of this logic in the breeding and treatment of sick guinea-pigs. We saw how guinea-pig meat is transformed into a 'curative' meat because of its general nutritive properties. Food, as a source of energy and a 'vital reproductive force', helps maintain and re-establish the internal equilibrium of the body together with thermic and natural phenomena. *Desmando* illnesses also derive from excesses of hot or cold food, not only from the environment and from variations in daily temperature. One of the limitations of many empirical studies in Ecuador is that they separate medical anthropology from the anthropology of food and vice versa. The treatment of illness through diet is common in all varieties of popular medicine. In this respect we noted that the guinea-pig is 'hot' because of the intrinsic properties of its meat. I then went on to examine in more detail recipes and ways of cooking that are particularly recommended, as well as the relationship between food and specific types of illnesses. My point of departure is that roasting, frying or boiling guinea-pig meat shows us the different aspects of 'heat' associated with various illnesses and their therapies. In the next section I shall review some of our empirical findings.

The Consumption of Guinea-pigs and the Female Reproductive Cycle

The best way to begin this section is to introduce a food taboo: during her menstrual periods, a woman has to avoid eating guinea-pig meat since it can produce irritation and a greater loss of blood. Menstruation is not seen as a moment of 'weakness' of 'loss of strength', but as a process of 'renovation' and 'bodily cleansing', which should not be interrupted or hurried. Some female informants point out that it is better to eat guinea-pig when a woman's period has finished, 'just in case' there is a need to counterbalance excessive losses that are difficult to control. In the communities we have studied, there is no clear evidence that this advice is converted into common practice.

On the contrary, when the period does not come and a woman is pregnant, the ideal is to eat *locro* or a broth of guinea-pig 'very soon'. The idea is that this dish helps to ease the nausea of the first few months and gives 'energy' – 'much energy' – to the mother and the foetus. One of the constant concerns of our informants is not to 'lose strength', but to 'supply strength' during the pregnancy period. It is recommended that the guinea-pigs should be one year old, in other words fully 'mature' and 'hotter', and preferably cooked in soup. Pregnancy is obviously a crucial period in the reproductive cycle and it is therefore important to maintain energy equilibrium and the 'strength' of the body. Eating guinea-pig – the hottest meat – is compensated by a diet that also includes fresh food every day. However, during the period shortly before delivery, women are advised to stop eating guinea-pig meat. None the less, particularly in Indian communities, people believe that the consumption of the guinea-pig's stools – in very small quantity and mixed with eggs and water – helps women during delivery. Another 'magical' remedy consists in taking the fur off the female guinea-pig's buttocks, putting it onto a tin plate or any other cooking-vessel, roasting it first, and letting it boil. This infusion helps to ease delivery.

In Indian communities, the first food recommended to a mother after birth is a thick broth of guinea-pig. In Chismaute Telán, people particularly recommend using all the 'blood' of the guinea-pig for this broth so as to make it a stronger dish. Here there is a clear attempt to restore lost energy. After an interval of two or three days, the mother may be given chicken soup, although during this period she will still be fed with guinea-pig broth. However, this is not the 'ideal' practice as defined by our mestizo female informants. They advise starting with a broth of fresh meat, such as chicken or rabbit – if available – followed by beef and then by a *locro* of guinea-pig. Here the logic of providing 'easy digestion' and avoiding 'stomach irritations' is considered to be more important than the rapid replacement of energy lost in labour. In Chirinche, for instance, we found a very precise model which involves a series of *locros*: the first food might be a cool *locro* of chicken, then a less cool though still not hot *locro* of meat such as rabbit; then a hotter *locro* of lamb; then beef or pork; and finally a good broth of guinea-pig. People are recommended to repeat this weekly sequence for a month, and, if possible, to extend it for another two. The idea is that after 'so much effort' the replacement of lost equilibrium should not be done too suddenly, as this may cause a whole series of upsets in a weakened body. The passage from cold to hot needs to be handled slowly; a weekly diet of *locro* allows this to be reached.

In the period after birth, two weeks after delivery a woman can take up housework again as well as farming duties, such as helping in the house and taking an active part in sowing and weeding. The concept of a period after birth recognizes a set of complications, such as vaginal infections, cervicitis or salpingitis, which are common during the forty days after delivery. Muñoz Bernand (1986, pp. 196–8) classifies different forms of the period after birth as 'illnesses of God', in other words, of 'microbes' which can be treated with modern medicine. The idea is that the body of the parturient is still 'soft' and has only partially recovered, and is therefore exposed to further illnesses and 'relapses'. In some cases, 'temperatures', together with vaginal infections, bleeding and aches, can cause women to 'go mad'. When this is the case, as we found in Palmira Dávalo, it is important to immediately eat a simple soup of guinea-pig, fortified with milk, eggs and marrow. This diet has to be repeated at least three times in a row, and the diet may be extended for longer. In the mind of our informants, the efficacy of this 'diet of broths', mainly preventive, is unquestioned.

Let us conclude with a reflection about the 'debility' of women in general. Up to this point, I have developed the theme of loss of strength in the context of pregnancy and labour, where such loss really does take place. However, I believe that there is an underlying idea that a woman is more sensitive to cold than a man and that she is consequently more exposed to illnesses that derive from a loss of organic equilibrium caused by cold. Therefore, it is common to take special care to prevent women from eating cold food. The consumption of guinea-pig therefore guarantees an adequate dietary balance.

The idea of prevention is clearly embedded in the logic of a postnatal diet, since this period is crucial for the mother and the child because of breast-feeding. People believe that guinea-pig soup helps the mother to produce plenty of milk. There is a consensus about this in both mestizo and Indian communities: in order to produce more milk, women need to eat mainly hot food.

Finally, when the reproductive life cycle is over, with the onset of the menopause, we find again a *locro* diet where soup or the *locro* of guinea-pig is central. People also recommend preparing this dish without bleeding the animal and without washing it inside, as this makes for the transfer of more energy. Likewise, people advise eating stewed guinea-pig.

We have already seen several times that guinea-pig meat is considered to be hot, and consequently to have the property of transmitting heat to the person who consumes it. In the logic of humours and of hot/cold foods, excesses need to be avoided. Hence roasted guinea-pig is always served with potatoes, which are cool. Fried guinea-pig is even hotter, since oil and fat transmit more heat. The *locros* or soups, and stews, are boiled and are therefore less hot and heavy than the other dishes. Moreover, they are not served with the heavy and fatty sauces I described in the previous chapter. The underlying logic, here, is that the longer food is put in contact with water the cooler it becomes. Our female informants, when confronted with this problem, affirm that the longer a food is left to boil, the cooler it becomes. However, soups are eaten warm and are therefore never 'cold'. In the spectrum ranging from hotter to cooler foods, boiled food is obviously cooler than fried or roasted. Therefore, since people are searching for the transmission of energy and heat but good digestion is also a concern, in order to prevent diarrhoea or heaviness of the stomach soups, *locros* and broths normally constitute not only an ideal 'democratic', peasant food, but also fulfil therapeutic functions of considerable importance.[7] This can be seen clearly in the close relationship between guinea-pig broth and a woman's reproductive cycle, which I discussed above. I shall now develop further analysis of the broth or *locro* of the guinea-pig as 'ideally' curative.

Guinea-pig Meat and Illness: General Remarks

Guinea-pig broth is recommended for all types of disease. In this way, the guinea-pig is a part of therapy, but not the sole element, since people also use herbal treatments, as well as medicines bought in local chemist's shops. My main objective is to identify the role of the guinea-pig as a meat that has curative properties, rather than to analyse in detail the therapies and the agents who take part in them.

In the introduction to this chapter, we observed that the theory of humours is related to illnesses that have their origin in *desmando* (lack of control) and from lack of precautions in the face of natural phenomena. We should not be surprised, then, that guinea-pig broth is one of the best remedies for cold and the discomforts that come with it – temperature, general weakness, sweating and subsequent dryness. This is because it is immediately efficacious, since it is possible to 'sweat temperature' by taking a good quantity of very hot guinea-pig broth. In contrast to the logic of cooling – which derives from both variations of temperature and the cold winds of the sierra, and which is also the cause of many colds, throat infections and lung illnesses – there is a simple logic of heat. In this respect, other meats are recommended as well as that of the guinea-pig, such as pork and beef, as well as different types of herbs, which are used to prepare infusions. Estrella (1978, p. 78) mentions, among different herbs, *tipu*, *malico*, borage and scented mallow. It is also very common to be advised to take alcoholic drinks, such as *chicha* mixed with alcohol, lemon and salt.

By the same logic, guinea-pig meat should not be eaten when a sick person suffers from diseases that are caused by excessive heat moving from the outside to the inside of the body. Among these illnesses are malaria and yellow fever. But tuberculosis (TB) – normally identified as an illness caused both by microbes, by hard living conditions and by conditions of poverty – can be cured by rest, plenty of warm clothes and nourishing food such as guinea-pig broth (Estrella, 1978, p. 165). All these sicknesses are defined as sicknesses 'of God'.

In the light of these empirical findings, we can also observe a logic of opposites: a belief than when there are deep wounds that take time to heal guinea-pig meat should not be eaten. The logic is that there is a risk of infection because of raised skin temperature; consequently, the body reacts against everything that tends to 'irritate' it. Hot foods, among them guinea-pig meat, are considered to be particularly irritating and therefore highly counter-productive in treating wounds. Many of our female informants frequently pointed out that guinea-pig broth is recommended when someone suffers from acute and continuous headaches. However, there are disagreements, since headaches in themselves are not something that needs to be cured. Treatment is given only if other symptoms appear, such as neuralgia, vomiting and diarrhoea. In Indian communities in particular, it is thought that guinea-pig broth holds back vomit and prevents dizziness, so that it is advisable to take a good cup of the liquid before beginning a bus or lorry trip. The same is true of infantile diarrhoea, although there are also disagreements about this: on the one hand, people argue that liquid has to be taken to avoid the body drying out; on the other, people think there is a risk of irritating the stomach because the liquid is hot. We have also observed a variant of this broth where the final result, after a good deal of cooking, is not a soup but a sort of jelly of guinea-pig meat mixed with potatoes, which is given to a child affected by diarrhoea. There are two aspects: it is a dish which cures and feeds at the same time. We also find guinea-pig broth in almost every case of 'anaemia' or 'lack of blood', especially after bleeding from a wound haemorrhage and for women during the postnatal period. Acero Coral (1985, p. 32) points out that there are two versions of this soup: a normal recipe for adults, and boiled guinea-pig in cow's milk for children.

We have seen, then, that the guinea-pig broth, with variations, is a type of food that is central to almost all the treatments of illnesses of *desmando*. It is thus important to link food therapy to a wider logic of the humours, as I indicated in the introduction to this chapter. However, we have also seen that in the case of 'illnesses of God' guinea-pig becomes a curative meat. Therefore, the common element in these two logics is the need to produce and restore a balance of energy, since the disease has triggered off physiological processes that need to be brought under control. Likewise, in any case, it is important to remember that the guinea-pig, as a therapeutic food, is only one part of the whole treatment, which includes different types of herbs, modern medicines, rest and physical isolation. Since we are not writing a book on general medical anthropology, we have attempted a systematic presentation of those therapies only.

Before proceeding with the analysis of the illnesses 'of the country', which would mean leaving food and entering the world of 'ritual cleansing' and *sobada* (healing massage), I would like to mention the case of the *chuchaquis* – upset produced by excessive intake of alcohol. Peasant popular therapy includes guinea-pig as an ideal food for rebalancing the organism after a night of binges, heavy drinking and vomiting. In such cases, traditional guinea-pig broth is accompanied by roast guinea-pig with a traditional peanut sauce. This latter form is preferred, since people both acknowledge its therapeutic properties and consider it to be a finishing touch to the previous day's party. We should remember that roast guinea-pig is the 'dish of kings' in the sierra.

The Body of the Guinea-pig: Illnesses 'of the Country' and the *Sobadas*

As we have previously pointed out, illnesses 'of the country' are opposed to illnesses 'of God' in one major way: they only strike Indian people. Illnesses 'of God' are modern diseases, generated by 'microbes', and therefore attack everybody. This has secondary implications, which are important, since guinea-pig meat is used as a therapeutic food by both mestizos and Indians and in both rural and urban worlds. This 'therapeutic food' – if I may be allowed the metaphor – is only a small part of the knowledge and cultural practices that constitute the vast field of Ecuadorean popular medicine. On the contrary, *limpiadas, limpias, sobadas* and *sobas* using guinea-pigs are still much practised among Indian people, but only in exceptional cases among mestizos. Let us analyse this in greater detail.

The guinea-pig as a food is connected to the logic of humours. During the *sobada*, the whole body of the live animal is used at the beginning of the ceremony, as an instrument which makes it possible to read the illnesses that affect a specific patient. The guinea-pig is not only a meat, but meat and 'spirit' at the same time. Therefore it is a tool for investigation, which, in the hands of an expert, permits an early diagnosis of a disease. This is because of the idea that a certain mimesis exists between the patient and the animal, since the animal has a set of qualities that allows the transfer of symptoms. Before beginning a general analysis of illness, though, we need to examine a *sobada*.[8]

Sobadores (healing masseurs) can be either men or women and can treat a small clientele – their family, relatives and members of the community – or patients who come from further away because of their good reputation. Their prestige is mainly related to their experience and years of practice. The cost of a *sobada* varies accordingly to their status. Generally speaking, people prefer to do a *soba* with an experienced *sobador* who is not a relative of the sick person. Aguiló (1987, p. 172) has remarked on the belief that the result of the cure depends on the fee of the *sobador*, which has been agreed on beforehand. The *soba* is normally given in the patient's home, but can also take place in the house of the *sobador*. There is widespread agreement that Tuesdays and Fridays are the ideal days for this practice, since they are considered particularly auspicious. On those days, people believe that the *sobador* will receive particularly 'strong' help not only from saints and the Virgin, but also from the mountains.

The practices of the *soba* differ in some respects, which, from one point of view, may appear to be very minor. For instance, there is no agreement as to the size, the sex, the age or the colour of the guinea-pig that is to be used. Some informants say that it is better to use small guinea-pigs (between three weeks and one month) and of mixed colours. When people refer to colours, they usually consider no more than three, others only two. Yet others prefer guinea-pigs of one colour only – preferably black and fairly big. This is because the black animals 'suck' the disease out better. However, Aguiló (1987, pp. 171–2) explicitly points out that in the Chimborazo area the favoured kind of guinea-pig is the *malton*, not too young or too old, and with a white coat. Apparently white allows a better 'reading' of illnesses that have external manifestations. Sometime the size of the guinea-pig is associated with the age of the patient; in the case of children, small guinea-pigs are preferred; in the case of adults, bigger guinea-pigs are better. Gender is also taken into consideration, since some of our informants insist that a woman needs to undergo a *sobada* by using a female guinea-pig, a man via a male animal. In some cases, particularly with *maltones*, people say that the gender of the guinea-pig should be different from that of the patient. A guinea-pig of the same gender as the patient is recommended when the animal is younger than one month. These small variations, though, do not contradict a high degree of consensus in relation to the origin of the guinea-pig: it has to come from the patient's home. The proximity, the closeness and the mimesis, once again, guarantee that the *sobador* will be able to accomplish his/her task more safely and with greater efficacy. When the patient travels to the house of *sobador*, he/she is advised to bring with him/her the guinea-pig that is to be rubbed on to his/her body. Only in extreme cases can the *sobador* use his/her own guinea-pigs or, as a last chance, the animal can be purchased, either in the market or from a neighbour.

Secondly, there is disagreement about the best time for a *sobada*. Normally it takes place during the day, because the examination of the animal's organs is done better in daylight. However, for other informants, especially in Palmira Dávalo and Chismaute Telán, the best hour is at dusk – at six o'clock, just before sunset. Likewise, some informants told us, when the patient is very 'weak' or is thought to be affected by *cuychi*, it is better to do the cleansing at midnight. In serious cases, *sobadas* can or should be repeated several times, possibly at different times of the day or night. It seems, though, that both the relatives of the patient and the *sobador* are thinking of an auspicious time rather than simply a moment in the day when there is more light and better visibility. Finally, all these disagreements show variations in strategies and practices because people are really seeking for great precision in the diagnostic process. The *sobador* who has accumulated a lot of experience decides what steps to take in relation to the age of the patient and the type of illness for which he/she is consulted.

One or more close relatives of the patient are normally present at the *sobada*, especially when the patient is a child. The *sobada* is a ritual of diagnosis, which simply consists in rubbing the body of the patient with a live guinea-pig until the animal dies. The technique of rubbing varies: some *sobadores* prefer to do it with circular movements, others with vertical ones, some rub 'hard' from the beginning, others just at the end, when the guinea-pig does not whine any more. *Sobadores* allow themselves to be guided by the patient, who indicates, as precisely as possible (if his/her condition permits this), which parts of the body are in major pain. The *sobador* has to stop for a few seconds more to create a longer contact between the aching part and the guinea-pig. The patient may be clothed or naked, but it is always better to have direct contact between the guinea-pig and the parts attacked by the disease. The *sobada* is always performed with tobacco and alcohol. The *sobador* drinks and smokes, and then blows the smoke of the cigarette and the fumes of the alcohol continuously on the body of the patient. It is believed that tobacco and alcohol help the disease to 'leave' and 'pass on' to the guinea-pig. In many cases the process begins before the ceremony, since the *sobador* talks about the illness with the relatives and with the sick person, in order to elicit the origin of the symptoms, their duration, the length of time during which the patient has been affected and the treatment that has been given. During these talks, the *sobador* begins to smoke and drink unrestrainedly. When this happens in the hut, rather than outside, at the moment of the *sobada* the room will be impregnated with smoke and the smell of brandy. Some *sobadores* carry out the rubbing of the guinea-pig with a bunch of herbs, including rue, Santa Maria, mallow, artemisia and rosemary. At the moment of the cleansing, too, some experts prefer to stay in the room with only a relative or the person in charge of the patient. At the moment of rubbing, the *sobador* is helped by praying uninterruptedly, asking God and, eventually, saints and the Virgin for help.[9]

When the guinea-pig dies from asphyxia, the rubbing is over. Our impression is that the expert decides the time that it takes for the animal to die. Generally speaking this process lasts between fifteen minutes and a long half-hour. Obviously, at the beginning, the animal whimpers and grunts, but only for a few minutes. Then, once it has passed away, the process of diagnosis begins. The guinea-pig is normally cut into halves, and after taking out the entrails, a careful examination of the organs takes place, which aims at identifying the disease. It is important to remember that the *sobador* reads, sees and observes certain signs, some of which are ambiguous. Therefore the animal is nothing more than an instrument, an 'aid' in the process of interpretation and diagnosis. Moreover, we should remember that the *sobador* is in possession of a set of data which were given to him/her, in many cases, by the sick people themselves or by their relatives. The guinea-pig consequently enables people to 'objectify' a set of hypotheses that the expert has gathered beforehand. For these reasons, the *sobada* may be considered to be a sort of 'primitive X-ray'. However, the *sobador* is consulted only for certain types of illnesses. A disease, then, may be categorized in the first place by the relatives of the patient and by the patient himself. The question which then arises is the 'fit' between this initial interpretation and the authoritative 'voice' of the expert. The social process that is triggered off highlights a sequence of ideas and practices that belong to the same semantic and culturally codified field. This allows a certain degree of juxtaposition of diagnoses, since the *sobador* confirms or refutes an intuition that exists in the mind of the relatives and some of the patients.

This reasoning leads us to our central theme – which diseases are treated with *sobadas*? Aguiló (1987, p. 172) points to cases where the disease is mainly caused by *huayra* (illness of the wind), which call for a consultation with a *sobador*. Muñoz Bernand (1986, pp. 196–8) regards 'cleansing' as a central part of the treatment in the case of illnesses 'of the country', and also of 'bad' illnesses – in other words, where there is a suspicion of evil eye or of wrongdoing. Barahona (1982, p. 146) gives a list that includes both the diseases 'of the country' – those which are engendered by evil eye – and also certain diseases 'of God' such as measles and flu. Acero Coral (1985, pp. 16–24) also mentions the *huairashca* (*mal aire* or *mal herido*). Estrella (1978) differentiates between the illnesses 'of God' and 'of the country' and only introduces 'cleansing with the guinea-pig' as part of the diagnostic process for the following diseases: 'fright' (*susto* or *huashashungo*); *mal viento* (sickness of the wind), *mal de aire* ('air sickness') or *huayrascha*; *mal blanco* (the white disease), *mal de caballo* ('disease of the horse') or *brujeado*; and finally the disease of the 'rainbow' or *mal del cuichi* or *cuichig-unguy*. Balladelli (1988, pp. 231–7) points out certain symptoms that refer to both diseases 'of the country' and diseases 'of God'. None the less, 'cleansing' with the guinea-pig appears to be particularly important in the diagnosis of *mal viento*, *susto* and *mal de calle* (sickness of the street) – prototypes of diseases 'of the country' – and in the *colerin*, which is a disease 'of God' produced by emotional disequilibrium. McKee (1988, pp. 222–3) has found that 'cleansing' by guinea-pigs is done when people think that a child with diarrhoea is suffering from 'illness of the wind'. Aguirre Palma (1987, p. 85) links 'illness of the wind' to illnesses such as pneumonia, tuberculosis, 'fright', headache and vomiting, which can be cured through cleansing with a guinea-pig.

Our findings confirm this: the *sobada* mainly takes place when the relatives of the patients or the patients themselves think that they have been attacked by the illness 'of the country'. None the less, this practice is declining in mestizo communities. The *sobada*, like diseases 'of the country' is seen as a hangover from 'backwardness' and 'primitivism'. The conceptual world of mestizo people is still be found, to a certain extent, even in the epoch of 'modern' medicine. People still believe in the magical effects of particular supernatural phenomena and have a very practical knowledge of traditional herbal medicine. We can observe a similar process in the impact of evangelical religion in Palmira Daválos. One of our informants spelled this out rather frankly: 'today there are doctors, nurses, we go to hospitals, and nowhere else'.

In Indian communities, where the *sobada* is still carried out and where *sobadores* are available at both local and regional levels, we have found a strong predominance, in cases of 'cleansing', of the illnesses 'of the country'. Although there are no longer traditional healers in Chismaute Telán, it is customary to consult them on the day of the market at Guamote. On this day there are at least eight traditional healers; many of these follow their clients closely and some are able 'to do the cleansing' in order to diagnose diseases. Muñoz Bernand, enquiring about the common attributes of illnesses 'of the country', writes as follows:

> normally we think that these are caused by the 'illness of the wind', but this term is found also in other contexts . . . the air of these illnesses is not the cold wind of *desmando*, but corresponds more to steam or to an imperceptible smell, which is why it represents a danger . . . This general idea of hazardous exhalations is not separated from concrete experience since some symptoms are attributed to 'antinomies', such as diminishing eyesight, trembling and skin rashes that are really associated with mephitic and mineral exhalations . . . The antinomies are fumes, gas or exhalations, not only in the strict sense of air which is taken in, but also in a metaphorical sense, which includes, flashes and thunders, lightning and rumbles. (1986, pp. 138–9)

Natural phenomena such as the 'rainbow' or *cuichig*, the *mal aire* or *huayrashca*, therefore, belong to this conceptual world and are particularly emphasized by our informants. The 'rainbow' is not only thought of as a concrete phenomenon but also has properties 'concealed' in specific places in the mountains, in still water or in particular ravines, all of which should always be avoided. Other informants pointed out the importance of avoiding some places at particular times of the day, such as dawn, midday, dusk or midnight. These attacks produce diffuse muscular aches, serious depression, passivity and the appearance of pimples and malignant growths. When it strikes women, it can make them pregnant, or, in the case of young women already pregnant, can cause their death or the malformation of the child. The *sobada* provides an accurate diagnosis, and when used promptly can prevent an illness from developing. For many people, *huayrashca* is very serious and even fatal. Some informants say that the *cuichig* is like a 'spiritual' and sexual force, since it is particularly attracted by young women who wear bright clothes. Faced with the prospect of an attack, the *sobador* will look on the guinea-pig's back for a gleam 'like water on oil', which is an indication of an attack of the 'rainbow'. This has to be done before beginning to rub. When there are strong suspicions, midnight is the best hour for carrying out the ceremony. Another important sign is when the guinea-pig takes a long time to die, even if it is rubbed hard. Since this is a generalized disease, which attacks the nerves, the *sobador* will try to carefully inspect the organs of the animal in order to find out which have been affected. Particular attention is paid to its size, to the colour and to the presence of blood. Lastly, the presence of yellowish 'swellings' on the neck is also a clear sign of the attack of *cuichig*. Once the diagnosis is done, the healing process begins, through the use of herbs and the cleansing of pimples. Moreover, the *sobada* is a *limpia*, a process of bodily purification. The guinea-pig, then, enables people to verify a diagnosis, but, since it also 'sucks' the disease, it therefore helps the sick person to recover. Some informants mentioned to us that, under these circumstances, it is better to repeat the 'cleansing' two or three times during the two weeks that follow the first treatment by the *sobador*.

The *mal aire* or *huayrashca*, is caused by the noxious exhalations I mentioned above. They are present in nature and are found in marshes, ravines, wells and particular mountains. Mountains have a special significance in Ecuadorean Indian culture: the admiration and adoration of mountains is mixed with a deep fear of malevolent forces, which set off diseases and even death (Moya, 1981, pp. 58–61). However, some informants do not associate 'illness of the wind' with mountains and ravines, but with very concrete phenomena, such as strong and sudden winds, storms and hurricanes. Aguiló has observed that in Chimborazo people attribute the *huayra* with all the characteristics of live and autonomous beings. He writes:

> The *huayra*, though not the antithesis of the Pachamama, but rather a secondary and inferior being, is seen as the incarnation of an evil spirit, the *supay* (devil), which is a malignant deity for Quichuas and Aymarás. It is for this reason that its presence automatically induces terror and dreadful anguish . . . people who have been caught by whirlwinds are

inexorably affected by the *huayra-unguy* (sickness of the air), which requires the intervention of the traditional healer to get rid of it. (1987, p. 19)

This illness produces a thermic imbalance – a strong internal, cold feeling. This physical condition normally entails acute headache, abnormal temperature, internal infection, vomiting and diarrhoea. Likewise, the ill person becomes depressed, 'keeps silent' and feels 'fear and anguish'. The *sobada* helps in diagnosis and in purification. 'Cleansing with an egg' is similarly widely employed. Some of our informants believe that its efficacy is the same as that of the guinea-pig, while others argue that the guinea-pig is more effective and appropriate. In order to diagnose *mal aire*, the *sobador* uses as an indicator the span of time that the animal takes to die: if the animal dies quickly, it is thought that illness is present. When the animal is dissected and many of its organs seem to be affected and swollen – with strange coloration and with a lot of blood or spots on the heart – it means that the animal has been struck by an 'attack of *mal aire*'. Even in this case, the *limpia* is seen as a process that begins the process of healing and consequently has to be repeated several times in the week following the first treatment. *Mal aire* is an illness that strikes indiscriminately and is particularly dangerous for children, as they die more easily. If the curing process is not successful after the first *limpias*, people advise taking the patient to the doctor or to the nearest health centre.

Another illness 'of the country' is *espanto* – a sudden fright which induces emotional upsets that stimulate the development of the disease. The signs of this disease are, as in the previous one, neuralgia, loss of appetite, vomiting and diarrhoea. 'Fright' particularly strikes those children and adults who, for one reason or another, are very weak. The *sobador* takes part in the diagnosis, but can only heal if he/she is an experienced *curandero*. The cure of 'fright' requires a set of rituals that are carried out after the diagnosis, although I shall not discuss them in detail here. The diagnosis of 'fright' is particularly difficult, and different signs are used to detect it: the guinea-pig has to die quickly; the entrails must be carefully observed to see whether there are any spots; the heart has to be examined to see whether it, too, is spotty (particularly white spots); last, but not least, the nervous system of the animal has to be checked before a *sobada* of an animal that is very excited before the beginning of the ritual – a clear sign that it is probably a case of 'fright'. Balladelli (1988, pp. 324–5) reports two signs in particular: the presence of a membrane in the large intestine which, when dipped into water, reflects light like a mirror; and, after the *limpia*, when the animal is skinned and immersed in water its body and legs still tremble.

When people are suspected of evil eye, because they are envious of neighbours or relatives, the option of consulting the *sobador* is available, but, in the opinion of our informants, it is better to go to a very experienced *curandero*. However, some informants refer to 'sickness of the street', 'sickness of the horse' or 'white sickness' as typical cases of spirit possession. Therefore, they normally advise 'cleansing' the body, which includes the use of the guinea-pig as one option – though not the one most commonly recommended.

In any case, once the *sobador* has defined the illness, he/she has to create a distance from the animal that has been used. The idea is that the animal, since it has sucked out the disease, can be contagious and therefore has to be carefully put on one side. The *sobador* normally throws it away in a particularly well-hidden spot and comes back to the *sobador*'s house without turning back. If he/she does otherwise, he/she is in danger of catching the illness that has just been extirpated. Likewise, once the ceremony has finished, the expert has to return home using a different path, possibly being taken there by a guide. The function of the guide is to warn him or her if they are likely to meet anybody on their way. If this happens, the guide has to whistle or make an agreed sign, so that the *sobador* can hide. It is believed that, if somebody sees the *sobador*, the process of curing which has recently started could 'get lockjaw'. Where this belief is strong, we found a parallel idea that the best moment to perform the ceremony is at midnight, since at that time the chances of the *sobador*'s being seen are much less.

Minor Curative Properties of the Guinea-pig

The curative properties of the guinea-pig go beyond food and the *sobada*. One set of beliefs concerns the properties of the faeces, blood, urine and bile of the guinea-pig. Most of them are 'beliefs of the past', which are not frequently put into practice today. This obsolescence is due, in part, to the penetration of modern medicine and, in part, simply to the fact that they have not been transmitted to the younger generation. However, our ethnographic data show that guinea-pig fat, produced when the animal is fried, is used in easing the extraction of thorns, in helping to heal particularly serious wounds and for rubbing parts of the body affected by rheumatism.

We also found a set of therapeutic practices for animals, in which the guinea-pig plays a major role. It is customary in some Indian communities to prepare guinea-pig broth to relieve fatigue and weakness among horses and cattle (when the animals are said to be 'becalmed'). A whole guinea-pig is boiled – without extracting the entrails – in a casserole, using onions, plenty of garlic and some pepper. When the guinea-pig is completely reduced, a thick broth is obtained; this is then allowed to cool down. The sick animal is then made to drink this broth. Initially, we were told, 'in the time of our elders', people used to mix the blood of a guinea-pig with roasted barley, to which salt was added, and this was given to the animals. In both of these practices the idea is that the guinea-pig gives 'strength' and 'helps the animal to recover'.

Conclusion: the Curative Use of the Guinea-pig as a Social Process

The diagnostic process and the initial stage of cure in traditional Indian medicine do not rely exclusively upon the guinea-pig. The use of the guinea-pig and the cultural practices associated with this animal cover a wide spectrum, but are not necessarily predominant. The *sobada* is undoubtedly a ritual instrument of great importance. Its survival depends not only on the transmission of relatively complex ideas, but also on the real possibility that the illnesses 'of the country' can recur many times. Moreover, we should not forget that the illnesses 'of God' point both to contact between Indian and mestizo worlds and to the influence of modern medicine in conceptualizing the process of illness and health. Modern medicine already exists as an available alternative throughout the sierra, and in many areas overlaps with a wider system of knowledge and practices where different aspects coexist.

The results of the *sobada*, as of all traditional medicine, depend upon the existence of an interconnection between the 'knowledge of the expert' and the 'knowledge of the layman'. Our data have been gathered from a layman's perspective and not from the perspective of an expert. In other words, our findings are clear

evidence of a shared understanding that is accepted by different
social actors in the 'informal' health system. In the case of *sobada*,
it is obviously important to have patients and relatives who firmly
believe in its efficacy, since the logic of the classificatory system
of the diseases 'of the country' is part of a cosmology ruled by the
importance of natural phenomena. These may set off uncontrolled
processes, accidents in people's lives, which, consequently, have to
be counterbalanced. Moreover, the *sobada* is carried out in the
context of a dialogue between the *sobador* and the people present
at the ceremony. It is usual that the *sobador* gives the results of his/
her analysis, but that others present can also express their
comments and opinions. The diagnosis, then, is nearly always the
product of an agreement between experts and laymen.

We have pointed out that many illnesses 'of the country' are the
result of real 'accidents' or arise from imprudence, since they could
have been avoided if people followed strict norms of conduct. The
cycle of health–illness–health, in this context, is mainly a social
process. *Sobadores*, like *curanderos* – who are able to treat 'evil eye'
– begin the process whereby the attempt is made to re-establish
social and cultural normality and to bring about the recovery of
the patient.[10]

Likewise, there are cultural variations according to ethnic and
religious boundaries. The difference between Indian and mestizo
cultures relates to the shift from using the guinea-pig as a
therapeutic food to using it as an instrument for diagnosis and
purification. I have tried to demonstrate that this is linked to
different ideas and systems of interpretation of illness and of
various kinds of physical and psychological damage. In the case
of illnesses 'of the country' – in other words, quintessentially Indian
sicknesses – the guinea-pig is seen not merely as food, but as
possessing a set of magical and instrumental qualities, which partly
relate to the animal's proximity to the patient. This proximity
is undoubtedly central to an understanding of the practical and
symbolic efficacy of the *sobada*. Mimesis derives not only from
contact, but also from the special properties of guinea-pig, since
the *limpia* is not done with any animal, after all. These are some
of the comments: 'it is a special animal'; 'it lives in the house'; 'it
has been living with people for long time'; 'it is a very well-known
animal'; and 'it is a favoured animal'. Without these ideas, the
'cleansing' of the body could not take place.[11]

In parallel, diseases 'of the country' imply a cosmology in which *aires*, exhalations, 'smells', *fulgores* (lightning) and *ruidos* (thunder) are forces that cannot be controlled, and which therefore need to be respected, because they are part of a shared world. Mestizo peasants show particular respect for these phenomena, but the potential danger caused by them is interpreted through a strict logic of hot and cold. Indians use these elements within a much wider system of interpretation, which includes their historical past, the weight of tradition and the contemporary social context. In their relationship to these natural elements, they infer a behavioural logic which seeks to avoid excesses that derive – as we showed earlier – from extreme ambition, from envy, from 'engagement without limits' and from receiving without being able to give in return.

Finally, the transition from Catholicism to Protestantism also entails a shift in perceptions of health and disease. Our informants in Palmira Dávalo show particular pride in stressing the difference between 'primitive' times and modern, current times. Evangelical influence is also evident, since they regard illnesses 'of the country' as belonging to a world that is ruled by the Devil and by black magic. However, nowadays there are 'pills, X-rays, injections and syrups'. A shift from 'deception' to 'light' has taken place.[12]

Notes

1. See especially Anderson (1980). There is no systematic study of Ecuador that accounts for existing variations in the system of classification. Fuentealba (1985), Heras *et al.* (1985) and Balladelli (1988) suggest a list of foods classified as cold and hot in different places in the Ecuadorean sierra. Generally speaking, there is most consensus about meat and such major products as potatoes and different kinds of maize. To illustrate disagreements, as well as local and regional variations, between these studies, a few examples will suffice: Fuentealba (1985, p. 184) finds that the sweet potato is hot, while Heras *et al.* (1985, p. 211) classify it as cool. The same happens with beans: Fuentealba (1985, p. 185) reports that they are cool; Heras *et al.* (1985, p. 212) say that soft beans are temperate and dry beans cool; Balladelli (1988, p. 456), on the other hand, says that soft, cooked beans are temperate, while dry cooked beans are hot and

different types of roasted beans are particularly hot. This last discrepancy also shows that there is a methodological problem in collecting data, since there are different types of beans, and their qualities can vary in accordance with the type of transformation they have undergone via cooking. At the same time, a clear and sharp distinction between hot and cold conceals the fact that there is in reality a spectrum between these extremes, in which some foods are classified as 'temperate' and others as 'cool', therefore nearer to hot or cold. In some cases, informants distinguish between the hot and the very hot.

2. Friedberg (1985, p. 142) points out that, in treatises on popular medicine in Bali, the classification of curative plants is so precise that each part of the plant – fresh, temperate or hot – can be used in a variety of ways. To my knowledge, there is no such refinement of classification in Ecuador.

3. See Muñoz Bernand (1986, p. 190) and Foster (1978). Foster has worked systematically on humoral theory and on the impact of cold and hot logics in popular medicine (1953, 1979). See also Currier (1966), Logan (1972, 1973) and Bougerol (1985). Anderson (1980) contains a useful bibliography for those who wish to explore the subject further.

4. Muñoz Bernand writes:

> Different diseases which are considered natural share common features, even if there are considerable differences in their aetiology. These are the ideas of infringement and of the guilt they engender. Infringement can be observed at different levels. In thermic and emotional *desmando*, the sick person infringes individual physiological and anatomical norms. In illness 'of the country' an offence against cultural norms of Indian society takes place – the taking over of a *religious* space considered unsuitable for humans – the profanation of pre-Columbian tombs; or breaks in the equilibrium between the mountains and crops. Illnesses 'of God' are punishments that, generally speaking, affect Indian people . . . which mark the infringement of a norm that in some cases has a divine status – the Indian lives in poverty because of his original sin. In others cases, it has a social nature – the Indian has to be subjected to the white person. (1986, p. 194)

5. It is interesting to observe that Muñoz Bernand (1986) does not pay special attention to food habits as part of therapeutic practices in Pindilig.

6. The findings of Bougerol (1985) about the Isle of Guadeloupe in the Caribbean clearly follows this line of enquiry. Even if we lack

systematic information about urban Ecuador, those who have lived for a certain period in Quito are still surprised by the special concern expressed by its inhabitants about changes in temperature and about cold as something 'exceptional'. At the same time, this coexists with marked 'endurance' to and tolerance of cold at home.

7. Undoubtedly, soups constitute the essence of Ecuadorean cooking in the sierra. The variety of recipes and the combination of vegetables, meat and cereals are rich indeed. A soup (*locro* or *colada*) is a meal in itself. The *fanesca*, served during Easter week, is the best illustration of this point, combining soft beans, fresh maize, fresh beans, peas, pumpkin, squash, cauliflower, onions, rice, garlic and peanuts with dried fish (cod, preferably the Norwegian type) in a rich combination of taste and of exquisite and delicate flavours and colours. Sánchez Parga (1985, p. 261), discussing the importance of soup in Ecuadorean highland cooking, calls it a 'matrix' which not only determines the food to be eaten, but also helps to establish a hierarchy of 'value-taste'.

8. Barahona's (1982) description of a *sobada* is still very relevant even if he discusses the topic in general terms.

9. Balladelli transcribes the testimony of a traditional doctor from Pesillo about the *sobada*:

> It is customary, for instance, for the guinea-pig firstly to be cleaned. For instance, I get a guinea-pig and its body is cleaned with guinea-pig. To clean it I would say to it 'Father, Son, and Holy Spirit, in the name of the Father, the Son and the Holy Spirit. In the name of the Father'. Clearly one has to carry on cleaning with the guinea-pig. Then 'Jesus, Jesus, Jesus is cleaning it. We are all brothers, Jesus is cleaning'. This word is mine: Jesus, you are cleaning, curing your children which we are. Heal the illness of your fellow-men, of your children. (1988, p. 236)

This text clearly shows the relationship that exists between the expert, the guinea-pig as an instrument and divine help. His testimony continues as follows:

> The guinea-pig cleans its body in this way, so you can see it all instantaneously. The whole illness comes out there, whether it is *mal de calle*, a fright or a temperature. For example when I cleanse a seriously sick person – children or infants – I open the guinea-pig and can then see the whole illness, which I can explain to any doctors who come to see the guinea-pig. I think 'Let's see whether he understands.' So . . . he understands X-rays and books, but he does not understand guinea-pigs. For instance, in the case of my

guinea-pig, I understand its changes: if it is well, frightened, or if it has cholera, cerebral fits, or if it has a heart attack: I can see everything, really everything: here it is! The diagnosis comes out better with the guinea-pig than with a candle. It is clear that is possible to see, to see something, by using a candle, but not as well as when using guinea-pigs. Because with the guinea-pig, it is like seeing the body of somebody, as if it was open. That is the way it is. (1988, p. 237)

This refers to practices in which a *sobada* with a guinea-pig is complemented by 'cleansing' done with a candle and/or an egg. Many *sobadores* – when they use the latter – ask to examine the urine of the sick person.

10. Muñoz Bernand (1986, p. 194) has observed that 'healing does not mean regression to the initial state, but bringing about a new regulation of the organism'. However, this 'normality' has changed because the organism has gone through the experience of illness. Disease can be seen as a sort of ritual of initiation, in which – among other things – a model of cultural interpretation of individual and social realities is confirmed.

11. The Indian peasant world is populated by benevolent and malevolent animals. The guinea-pig, as we might expect, is one of the most benevolent animals that can be found. Its malevolence only appears after a *sobada*, as we saw above. The proximity of the guinea-pig allows its behaviour, movements and grunts to be used as 'oracles'. It is possible to read thereby the coming of frost or of unexpected rain, or that somebody in the house or some cherished relative will fall ill, as well as unexpected visits. Generally speaking, this behaviour is only found among old guinea-pigs. People do not expect *maltones* to be oracles. It is important to remember that the guinea-pig is not the only animal which has these qualities. Bad omens and bad news can be seen in the behaviour of hens, of runaway cattle, of horses which rear up or in sheep which whistle (Aguiló, 1987, pp. 32–3). All these ways of 'coding' an event have been reported from Indian communities in Chimborazo.

12. Muratorio writes:

When evangelicals talk about their religious conversion, they refer back to their past experiences of 'living like animals' and use expressions such as: 'We were like dogs', or 'like savages', 'like beasts'. Self-control and the fact that they see themselves as free from behaviour which is now considered 'degrading' constitute the basis of a new self-respect and personal dignity. One peasant expressed this concept in the following words: 'If I do not behave as an animal, I can love myself and therefore I can reject those who despise me and call me "Indio".' Ideologically this new image embodies a form of protest, a rejection of old relations of exploitation in which Indian people were actually treated as 'pack-animals' and as 'subhumans'. (1982, p. 87)

CHAPTER SIX

The Meat as Commodity

In previous chapters, we saw that the production of guinea-pigs takes place within a set of social relations that govern both consumption and circulation, since guinea-pigs are exchanged within a system of offerings, which emphasizes the social relevance of religious feasts and political ceremonies and the status of those who take part in them. I have also tried to show that the guinea-pig – especially in Indian culture – is used in healing rituals. Moreover, I have tried to show how different ways of preparing guinea-pigs, based on humoral theory, which is still present in Ecuador, are fundamental in the treatment of particular diseases. Guinea-pigs are present, therefore, in nearly all socially important activities in individual as well as community life. The degree of 'social and symbolic saturation' of the guinea-pig, then, derives from its twofold nature: on the one hand, as 'use value', for immediate and direct consumption by producers; on the other, as a 'gift', intended to enhance the moral qualities of those who give and those who receive.

In a world of multiple transactions and exchanges, the guinea-pig does not appear to belong to a market economy or to have an 'abstract' price ruled by supply and demand. Some anthropological writings tried to separate – sometimes in a dualistic way – use value from exchange value; monetary relations from non-monetary ones; and goods given as presents from those which are bought.[1] The temptation to end our account there is strong. We might have concluded that the guinea-pig belongs to a 'precapitalist', 'traditional', 'magico-religious' world governed by rules that are disappearing with the development of capital relations in Ecuador. However, the world of the guinea-pig is more complex than this dualistic logic would imply as method of analysis.

In peasant economies, in general, and in Ecuador in particular, the majority of use values produced are also exchange values. In other words, the same products are both 'food' and 'commodities', since they are exchanged in both worlds: the world ruled by symbolic innocence and unselfishness, and the other, ruled by 'nasty materialist accumulation'. Nobody would deny that, in Ecuador, capitalist relations are predominant and that well before agrarian reform began land and labour flowed freely on the market as commodities. On the other hand, both in the past and in the present, peasants have experienced an intense process of migration as well as different modes of involvement in business relations. The need to gain money has been, and still is, a 'social' need which guarantees the reproduction of the productive process as well as reproduction in general. However, this does not imply that 'socially necessary labour time' on the part of producers determines the price of products once they reach the market. This is because the monetarized logic of reproduction is not determined by the logic of capital accumulation. Monetary capital is therefore less important than two other components which are part of the broader productive process – land and labour. This dynamic influences the relationship between subsistence and mercantile logic, so that primary products sold in the market constitute not only a 'real' surplus, but a surplus that is dictated by unfulfilled social needs, both within units of production and outside them, by the allocation of free services by the state. We shall now examine the productive strategies of the communities we have studied. It will then be much easier to see the role of the guinea-pig in market relations.

The Logic of Production and the Logic of the Market

I shall begin with the mestizo world. Tigualó, in the district of Salcedo, is a community of small landowners, where there is, however, a certain amount of economic differentiation, since some families possess land near the River Cutuchi. This enables them to obtain high yields of alfalfa on small plots of land. For all producers, alfalfa is a fundamental crop, which is used for feeding cattle – usually between two and five animals. Consequently, the daily sale of milk – between eight and fifteen litres – is the main source of monetary income. The production of maize, together with runner beans, is central for subsistence, even though this fodder is sometimes mixed with green (unripe) maize. Vegetables are also produced for internal consumption in small family orchards, together with maize and beans. It is important that legumes are rotated with these crops – barley, for example, is rotated with alfalfa. Guinea-pigs, together with less important animals, such as pigs and rabbits, are a major component of this diet, as well as milk and home-made cheese. Generally speaking, agricultural tasks are carried out by hand, although sometimes yokes of oxen are used on bigger fields. From the point of view of productive inputs, people buy improved seeds of maize, beans and peas, but do not use chemical fertilizers. Tigualó is a community that has been steadily losing its young labour force, which hardly ever comes back to the community except to take part in major celebrations. This migration, then, is really permanent, not governed by agricultural cycles, as in other communities in the sierra. The demographic impact of migration and pressure on the best land partly explains the development of relations of partnership in the community, when land is divided up into shares. Tigualó is linked to the market through relationships established during the important weekly fair at Salcedo.

Ayanquil, in the area of Quimiag and Penipe, in the province of Chimborazo, is also a small landowners' community, where land is subdivided into plots between one and two hectares in size. Nevertheless, producers have easy access to high-altitude moorland on the plateau, which remains communal apart from a few plots. This makes possible the development of a productive strategy based on an efficient mixture of agriculture and cattle-breeding. Consequently, the relative abundance of pasture makes it possible to raise cattle and sheep for sale in the market. The abundance of pasture explains the fact that nearly all families have yokes of oxen that are used to carry out farming activities. The hub of agricultural production is maize, which is cultivated together with beans and pumpkin. Normally there is an overproduction of beans – both the canary variety and red beans, both produced for the market. Apple and peach trees are also cultivated in considerable quantity, together with beans, again mainly for the market. Some highland families also grow potatoes, both for internal consumption and for the market. This diversification therefore requires a fairly permanent labour force. In Ayanquil, though, permanent or seasonal migration is only a marginal phenomenon. The sale of surplus crops and animals takes place in the market at Riombamba and the fair at Penipe.

Sharván is part of the canton of Gaulaceo, in the Azuay province, and, like the other communities already mentioned, is mainly an area of very small landowners. The plots owned by the 'larger' owners were scarcely more than two hectares in size. However, the situation has changed dramatically and, at the time of our field-work, communal lands were in the process of being divided up into plots of eight hectares to a family. Agricultural production is based on the cultivation of maize and beans, both fundamental in peasant diet. Peas are an alternative crop when the first cycle is over. This crop is considered to allow the land to rest and to 'regenerate itself'. At the same time, orchards are kept well stocked with pulses and traditional vegetables, such as onions, tomatoes and carrots. To prepare the land, people use yokes of oxen, which are widely available, while the *minga* – reciprocated labour – is the most common method of harvesting. Herds and cattle are kept in upland pastures for family consumption, although sheep and wool surpluses are sold on the market. However, in the community of Sharván handicrafts are also important. Thirty families produce tiles, which are sold locally or in Gualaceo. Likewise there are at least fifty shoemakers working for businessmen in Gualaceo, making between ten and fifteen pairs of shoes a week for many months in the year. Last but not least, there is female work: in the community there are forty needlewomen, who sew already-cut shirts, and another thirty weavers, who knit woollen jumpers. In all these cases, raw materials are provided by businessmen in Gualaceo and Chordeleg. On the other hand, it is common for the head of the household and usually the young men to work on the sugar-cane plantations at harvest-time. They also try to get seasonal work on road projects or in building construction in Azuay. In Sharván, then, the main participation in the market is not through the selling of agricultural and animal produce but rather through wage labour and domestic handicraft production.

Chirinche Alto, in Salcedo, is a mixed community which began with the distribution of land in the 1960s. Social differentiation is now well advanced; we also observed that, together with small landowners, there was a large population of landless 'scroungers'. Access to highland pastures enables families to raise a few cattle and, in some cases, quite large flocks of sheep. We observed here, again, the combination of maize with beans and potatoes. Both the

maize and the beans are consumed, but large yields make possible
a surplus – normally of potatoes and beans – which ends up on
the market. The raising of flocks of sheep is a major task, since it
is an important source of cash. The overall economic reproduction
of Chirinche, though, depends, most of all, upon income from
wage labour in the building industry in both Ambato and Quito.
This is seasonal and very irregular. It is common for many migrants
to come back home at the weekend.

Llactahurco, as well as Salcedo, is an indigenous community that
has been able to preserve a certain degree of independence from
the hacienda system, because it has access to highland pasture and
irrigated land. Over time, this has made the consolidation of small
reproductive units possible, although they vary in size from two
to five hectares. Potatoes, beans and barley are the main crops.
These become part of a system of rotation, which begins with
potatoes, then barley and ends with beans. People use a good deal
of fertilizer in growing potatoes, and tractors hired from the
Ministry of Agriculture as well. In irrigated areas, it is possible to
cultivate potatoes every year, as well as alfalfa, which is used for
feeding animals. Fattening pigs is as important as raising sheep.
Cattle are used for milk and for producing fresh cheese, but cheese
is seldom sold. Barley and beans are usually kept for family
consumption. Sharecropping contracts are fairly well developed,
especially in potato production. The migration of young people is
considerable and tends to become permanent. However, it is not
unusual for young migrants to come back home to help their
parents during sowing and harvesting. The role of institutions such
as the town hall was once strong, although there was some friction
between mestizos in the village of Cusubamba and the Andean
Mission. But the political weight of such institutions has decreased,
since different sections of the community have accused some of
their representatives of having negotiated with Ministry of Agriculture officials the allocation of upland plots to individuals.

Guzo, an Indian community situated in the area of Quimiag, in
the canton of Riobamba, Chimborazo province, has been historically linked to a Jesuit-owned hacienda. Nowadays, the community,
composed of three hundred families, has increased its land
ownership as a result of agrarian reform. The soil is good, and
there is water for irrigation in the lower part, which makes possible
mixed farming. This expansion has consolidated land ownership
into plots, on average, of five hectares, in a relatively dynamic land

market. Productive strategies are clear: one plot is planted with
maize and beans, the other with potatoes and broad beans. At the
same time, people have well-stocked orchards and fruit trees. As
already mentioned, potatoes are also very marketable. The remaining crops are used for household consumption. The existence of
much communal land in the highlands has made possible the
rearing of sheep and cattle without difficulty. Fertilizers and
improved seeds are widely used, especially in the production of
potatoes and various types of beans. This is an area that attracts a
labour force from across the region during the weeding and harvest
seasons, especially in Penipe canton. Relations with the market in
Riobamba are also very strong and active.

The history of the constitution of the 'village' of Palmira Dávalos,
in Guamote canton, is complex although for reasons of space I shall
not discuss it in detail. Suffice it to say that Palmira Dávalos is a
typical 'residential community', made up of peasants who come
from various communities, where they still own land. The majority
of agricultural activities are in Letra, Chauzán, Totorillas and
Atapos, ten kilometres distant. In some cases, people cultivate
not only their own plots but also others, through sharecropping
contracts. Farming is often done using tractors or hired oxen. The
most common technique of cultivation is the parallel, not mixed,
sowing of rows of potatoes and rows of broad beans. Barley is also
part of the system of biannual rotation. In this case, as in those
already mentioned, surplus potatoes go to the market. In the
highland area close to Palmira Dávalos, men earn a fair amount
from making ponchos, belts and blankets, which they then sell to
mestizo businessmen who live in the villages. The selling of labour
power is especially common on milk-producing haciendas in
Machachi, in the province of Pichincha. Some people also go to
the coast, as well as to Quito, to work in building construction.

Chismaute Telán – our last Indian community – belongs to
Guamote canton, and is part of Chismaute Larcapungo. Despite
the fact that in principle every family has enough land to live on,
the sandy soil does not allow the production of a constant amount
of crops. One way to resolve this ecological crisis is through using
land via sharecropping, notably in Telán and in Larcapungo, the
main emphasis being upon animal production and, especially,
sheep-breeding. The wool is sold at the fair in Guamote, and
constitutes an important source of cash income. Crops that are
traditionally cultivated in the highlands are potatoes, beans and

barley. However, the hiring of tractors is becoming more frequent in Chismauate Telán, although oxen and the traditional mattock are still used. Moreover people have begun to produce onions for sale in the market, together with a surplus of potatoes and maize at the sowing season. Migration is high and the pattern is as in Palmira Dávalos; agricultural labour goes to Machachi or to the coast, and to temporary building construction in Quito. Likewise, we have observed some female migration, in carrying work, mainly in the market in Riobamba, Ambato and Quito, and in foodstalls – *comideras* – in fairs in neighbouring villages and towns.

Even if incomplete, this survey of productive logics clearly shows the coexistence of subsistence and market strategies within different units of production. Some products, such as potatoes, beans, peas and fruit, and sheep products, such as wool, seem to belong to both logics. Others belong to the traditional household economy, such as maize, which is used exclusively for family consumption and in some cases as a supplement in animal fodder. The polyvalency of those products can also be explained by the use of different ecological niches in the Ecuadorean sierra, which makes possible the combination of agriculture and animal production. The degree of interplay with the market varies with the type of product, especially with regard to the surplus that can be sold. The bigger the surplus – in Guzo, for instance – the less the necessity of entering the money economy by working outside the village for wages, especially when there is a labour surplus within the domestic unit. However, the existence of a labour market – local, regional, rural and urban – at times of labour shortage or of labour surplus, functions as a major and effective pole of attraction for surplus labour. The transition to cash-crop cultivation in a peasant economy reflects this type of integration, as well as the fact that people have to buy part of their inputs (seeds and fertilizers, in the case of beans, potatoes and barley), or sometimes have to hire tractors, and above all to buy food needed for basic consumption but not produced within the household.

The guinea-pig can be found in each of the communities we studied and in every house we visited. It is a domestic animal, considerably more domesticated than pigs or sheep, which are regularly sold in the market. Furthermore, many producers are aware that the guinea-pig is not readily available in food markets, and less available than other meat in fairs and animal markets. These empirical findings are backed up by the fact that the consumption and use of the guinea-pig are highly ritualized – as we have seen. This, though, explains the logic of the producer, but not that of the consumer. If we accept for a moment that there is no systematic 'supply' of guinea-pigs, this could be partly due to lack of effective 'demand'. Therefore, when we pay attention to supply and demand, we should ask ourselves what is the real effect of external consumption. What requires further analysis, then, is the dual nature of the guinea-pig – as use value and exchange value – in the context of demand at the regional level. Hence, it is necessary to compare the logic of the producer with existing market mechanisms.

The Conversion of the Guinea-pig into a Commodity

In Llactahurco, but only exceptionally and during the winter, people sell a few guinea-pigs in the fair of Cusubamba. At this fair, people buy and sell larger animals in the market and there are no *revendonas* (female traders) who specialize in buying and reselling guinea-pigs, as in other areas of the sierra. It is rare for female traders to come up to Pujulí to buy guinea-pigs. Therefore, over and above those kept for family consumption, guinea-pigs are sold to the people of Cusubamba for their family consumption. Another key point is price. When producers 'feel' that the price that buyers are willing to pay is very low, 'then it is not worth-while selling guinea-pigs'; 'they always say that they are thin and weak'. In all cases, selling is justified by an urgent need, by some problem, such as an unexpected bill which needs to be paid. People do not like to sell guinea-pigs and in many cases buyers who have come to the community can only buy guinea-pigs after some wheedling.

The same logic is found in Ayanquil. Guinea-pigs are only sold 'to cope with urgent needs' – when there is economic shortage or when the doctor has to be paid or medicines have to be bought. Just as pigs are fattened for sale and sheep are bred to sell wool, guinea-pigs 'are kept in the house' and when necessary are fattened to be sold in the market. The most common remark heard about them is that they are 'firstly for eating' and only later for selling. Guinea-pigs are sold in the fairs at Penipe and Riobamba at prices which vary from 130 *sucres* for the smaller ones to 200 for the biggest.

In Tigualó we have found a higher volume of sales, especially during the summer. Here the reason is clear – the female producers say that 'selling them' guarantees an income when there are no crops. During June and August, there may be economic shortages, and the ritual calendar is less intense. Our female informants observe that because there are no festivals they can 'just sell them' and later can rapidly breed some more. However, they insist that one should never be without a guinea-pig, because there should always be 'something in the house for a treat'. Only a few of our informants agreed with the idea that guinea-pigs can be raised simply for sale, although guinea-pig is 'useful', since it can be sold whenever there is a shortage or when 'there are a lot of them'.

People in Chirinche Alto and in Tigualó think in the same way – women come down to the fair at Salcedo, twice a week, when they need money to get other goods for their daily needs. This selling is conceived of as 'contingent', and the stock of guinea-pigs functions as a form of insurance when there is a shortage of sugar, salt or flour. However, the rate of selling is slower than in Tigualó. We shall come back to the characteristics of the Salcedo fair later on in the chapter.

In Palmira Dávalos, as in Chismaute Telán, guinea-pigs are only sold in cases of extreme necessity. Here people justify selling them primarily to meet medical expenses. They are sold in the fair at Guamote, in the animal square. The price varies, but the highest price, for the best animals, is 100 *sucres*. Finally, there is 'symbolic' selling in this community, which was not mentioned by other informants – 'selling off' animals after the death of the female owner ('when a wife dies all the guinea-pigs must be sold').

Up to this point, the data are consistent: guinea-pigs are sold only in case of 'necessity', so productive strategies are shaped by the existence of a 'market' with its prices. The guinea-pig is still an exchange value, exchanged and transformed within specific contexts. Therefore one can infer that possible changes in ceremonial cycles, as well as dietary customs, can influence changes in the hierarchy of existing preferences. From an economic point of view, we can also infer that higher prices can lead to a general increase in production. The evidence for the first hypothesis is, at present, negative. We shall turn to the second hypothesis later. The case of Guzo, an indigenous community that is undergoing something of an economic boom, introduces an economic variant which we shall discuss below.

In Guzo there are five women who accepted the technical advice put to them by rural development workers. This included – in addition to other measures illustrated in Chapter 1 – that the hutch should be outside the house, and that 'improved' Peruvian guinea-pigs should be introduced. Without exception, female producers chose to sell the 'modern' or *macabeo* guinea-pigs, which are more highly valued on the market. The 'homely' *criollo* and *sacha* guinea-pigs, though, are still bred in the home and destined for 'traditional' consumption. However, not long ago the *criollo* guinea-pigs were being sold in situations of 'scarcity'. Nowadays, in principle, there are no such acute shortages. Arguments about preferences in the consumption of domestic guinea-pigs are actually about the taste of meat: 'the *sacha* is better'. When it comes to the 'improved' guinea-pigs, people express their hope of selling them for a better price: the price of a *criollo* was 150 *sucres* as against 300 for a 'Peruvian' one. However, in Quimiag there is no market for these animals, so women were obliged to bring them to Riobamba market on Saturdays and Wednesdays. The Riobamba market seemed to be the only hope for the future, even though there was no fixed demand at local and regional levels. Therefore the strengthening of guinea-pig production as exchange value – as a good mainly directed to the market – depends not only on existing demand but on the day-to-day market situation at local and regional levels. It is clear that, given the existing schedule of preferences, in the communities we have studied, incentives for increased production demand, above all, greater 'specialized' production of 'improved' guinea-pigs as exchange value. In order to maintain this process over time, a demand has to be met, which may not yet exist, or, rather, an unsatisfied demand.

Demand for Guinea-pigs

In relatively important fairs, such as Guamote and Salcedo, and in the most important ones, such as Ambato and Riobamba, there is a considerable volume of guinea-pigs in the animal markets. Unlike agricultural products, such as potatoes and onions, and other animals, such as cattle and sheep, which are exchanged within well-defined vertical fields, each managed by 'specialists', the commercialization of guinea-pigs has not produced a separate market. We found no 'middlemen' or 'big businessmen' who buy dozens and dozens of guinea-pigs,[2] although the selling of the guinea-pigs, virtually without exception, is done in marginal areas in fairs and markets by traders who also buy hens and rabbits. When this happens, trade in poultry is more important than trade in other animals. In the case of guinea-pigs, there is a predominance of *revendonas* – mestizo women who buy in small quantities in order to sell them again the same day, or as soon as they can at nearby fairs. The practice of *arranche* ('snatching' of what Indian peasants bring with them to sell, using violence, and for low prices) does not seem to be as common as is the case with other products and animals. However, many of these *revendonas* have important clients: restaurant-owners in Ambato and Riobamba. The rest of the buyers – especially urban mestizos – normally buy only small quantities. Small-scale buying and selling between Indians also occurs when it has not been possible to sell two or three guinea-pigs to a *revendona*, while *revendonas* may buy and sell up to twenty animals a day at a fair. Even under these circumstances, the profit which can be made from guinea-pig is relatively small.[3] The possibilities of 'making a fortune' – as some potato and cattle traders do – are very slight in this type of trading. We estimate that the profit on each animal is not more that 20 *sucres*.

The most important market is that constituted by restaurants and food stalls, mainly during fair days. The *revendonas* therefore need to develop a clientele composed of the owners of such eating-places. Obviously, the clientele is limited, and in consequence the actual market is small. In Guamote, on Thursday, the day of the fair, roast guinea-pigs are sold in a cafeteria, together with chicken soup, and at a food stall close to the town hall. Not more than three dozen are sold, since guinea-pig in peanut sauce, at the time of our fieldwork, could easily cost up to 350/400 *sucres*. Cooked guinea-pig is undoubtedly a booming trade in Ambato and Riobamba – two booming centres in the business network of the central Ecuadorean sierra. We shall now examine the culinary activities that take place in these two towns.

In Riobamba, in España Street, there is a restaurant specializing in traditional dishes which serves roast guinea-pig with peanut sauce as the main course on Saturday, the day of the fair. This is 'the' place to buy roast guinea-pigs. We estimate that they sell around 120 guinea-pigs during the whole day, with a profit of nearly 100 *sucres* on each animal. The animals are generally bought on Tuesday, the main day of the fair. The owner of the restaurant 'fattens' the guinea-pigs over the last few days with plenty of alfalfa. There are also other cafes: one on 5th of July Street, one on Orozco Street, another at the intersection of Chile and Juan Montalvo Streets and a fourth at the corner of Pichincha and Olmedo Streets. The first is used by mestizo and Indian people who are attending the fair. As well as the attraction of the guinea-pig, the 'tavern' also sells a 'good brandy'. Guinea-pig meat is prepared with peanut sauce, the price varying according to size. It is sold only on Tuesdays and Saturdays, the days of the fair. The other places are patronized more by mestizos. The restaurant in Chile Street sells them also on Mondays and Fridays, but it 'takes orders' for any day of the week. Lastly, guinea-pig is not the only speciality, since people also go out to eat *caucara*, a sort of 'baked pork'. This tavern is very popular. I have to stress that our data show no restaurant selling guinea-pig in the area of the market. If this happens, guinea-pig is not cooked as a special dish, but together with fried pig. This means that guinea-pig is not sold in one piece, but chopped up and served without potatoes or peanut sauce. In Riobamba, where there are two or three more 'refined' restaurants, it is possible to 'ask' for a guinea-pig which is it not part of the set menu – a clear indication not only of the presence of guinea-pig meat in urban popular cooking, but also of the existence of a weekly market where up to four or five hundred guinea-pigs are consumed. Two restaurant-owners pointed out that, in principle, it is not difficult to find guinea-pigs, since 'there are always plenty on the market'. However they were sceptical about a possibility of expanding consumption, pointing out that guinea-pig is an 'expensive, fancy dish', 'more expensive than fried meat'.

Ambato is a mountain town where people also appreciate guinea-pigs. Its more famous restaurants are located close to each other in the Avenida de la Circunvalación. Here we recorded the highest price for roasted guinea-pig with potatoes and peanut sauce: 500 *sucres*. However, they are normally sold for half the full price in what is called 'a double' – in other words 'two good helpings with a side order'. But even at this price, guinea-pig, at least in res-taurants, is still more expensive than rabbit. These two restaurants sell guinea-pig every day except Monday. In Ambato, unlike Riobamba, it is possible to find several places that sell guinea-pig every day in different places. We should remember that in Ambato there are more than fourteen independent markets. Due to its regional role, there is a fair on practically every day of the week

(Hanssen-Bauer, 1982, pp. 73–4). Many of these eating-places can sell up to a dozen roasted and chopped guinea-pigs. A very traditional-style place is the 'tavern' on the Avenida del Rey and Obispo Riera, where roast guinea-pig is sold at a 'popular' price, together with other specialities of the sierra: the *runaucho*, which is a *colada* of pea flour made with the entrails of the guinea-pig; and the 'thirty-one', a dish of finely chopped tripe soaked in milk and served with peanut sauce and various herbs. Needless to say, the *ranaucho* is a very peasant dish. The size of the market of Ambato is, we estimate, double that of Riobamba. However, in a town of nearly 100,000 permanent inhabitants, at least 10,000 of whom participate, every day of the week, in these economic activities, the consumption of 800 or 900 guinea-pigs every week does not constitute a big market. Guinea-pig is still an expensive and special dish in Ambato.

Another important element which explains limits on demand is the lack of butcheries specialized in selling guinea-pigs. If people want to eat guinea-pig, they have to buy live animals and feed them for a few days to compensate for any possible loss of weight caused by being transported and spending time in the market. They then have to kill them or find someone who will do this in their house and who is experienced in slaughtering animals. For the urban mestizo, this option is not available. This, plus the considerable purchase of meat in supermarkets, limits the mestizo's 'taste for' guinea-pig. The alternative is a restaurant that offers traditional dishes.[4]

Conclusion: the Limits of the Guinea-pig as Commodity

It should now be clear that a weak, or at least limited, demand faces a supply with similar characteristics. The 'private' purchase of guinea-pigs for family consumption appears to be fortuitous, depending on fixed and well-defined days, notably ceremonial, the festival cycle and private family ceremonies, in an urban context in which guinea-pig is a food found in traditional-style restaurants.[5]

For 'Peruvian' guinea-pigs, market prices are nearly prohibitive, not only as food in restaurants, but also for family consumption. This argument is used to underline and explain the urgent need for increasing production, lowering prices and, eventually, increasing consumption. I do not, however, accept the logic of this argument: during our fieldwork, prices were a real obstacle to massive consumption. Guinea-pigs were confined to their 'destiny' as 'exceptional and "structured" food' as I argued previously. The fact that the guinea-pig is a 'use value' constitutes a major limitation on supply.

I might have concluded by saying that guinea-pig is a 'peculiar' food. But this, in the end, does not distinguish it from other commodities. Therefore, from an anthropological perspective, these 'peculiarities' constitute the centre of an analysis focused on finding out why its conversion into use value is limited. The different arguments used start from complex and superimposed logics. On the one hand, cultural arguments refer to 'taste' or 'cooking', 'the relationship between food and health care' and the 'ritual use of guinea-pigs in healing ceremonies'. On the other hand, there may be social reasons concerning 'social relationships of a vertical and horizontal nature', 'variations in local participation in the ceremonial system', 'the festival cycle which must be followed' and the 'establishment and confirmation of social status'. We can infer, too, that female 'status' and the shift from one technology to another, or the passage from use value to exchange value, imply a loss of prestige and the denial of a typically female ancestral practice. Finally, macroeconomic arguments can be used: the lack of a labour force or of productive resources; the fact that prices are 'low' and do not constitute an incentive to maximize production and productivity.

A discussion of these aspects in the next and final chapter will allow me to summarize some of our findings within a wider anthropological context, the aim being to understand broader processes of social and cultural change, including resistance and traditionalism. Our data suggest that there is no fixed, historical 'linearity' and that individuals move in different spheres, many of them marginal, which do not threaten society and the state. In their search to negotiate 'fields of power and influence', people need to find the controlling 'centre' and the resources of which it disposes.

Notes

1. Empirical data used by Parry and Bloch (1989) show that in rather different societies and cultures there is a sphere of activities that is ruled by interpersonal and highly competitive relations. One important theoretical conclusion is that it is not necessary to attribute these changes to the development of monetary relations or to the impact of money on pre-existing social relations. In monetarized situations, as in Ecuador, the guinea-pig, because of its dual character as a commodity, can circulate both as exchange value and as use value. This consequently generates a unique dynamic, since it is not possible to predict, with mathematical precision, when the guinea-pig will be converted into a mere and simple commodity. Naranjo (1986, pp. 292–3), for instance, has observed that in 1983 – the same period as our fieldwork – because of the high price for guinea-pigs, peasants in many areas of the province of Cotopaxi preferred to sell them rather than keep them for domestic use. This means that, in the case of goods and products which are both use and exchange value, conversion – in both directions – depends on a set of factors which one can recognize, but which do not lead to any predetermined or consistent result.

2. The work of Bromley (1975, 1976, 1978) is still a classic introduction to the understanding of the phenomenon of markets and fairs in Ecuador. The research of Hanssen-Bauer (1982) about onion markets in Ambato gives a sound methodological approximation of how fairs work. Following the circulation of products allows us to follow producers and businessmen in economic contexts, where specialization makes the social links that lie behind any business transaction more visible.

3. It is important to recall that for many of our informants the largest sale of guinea-pigs occurs on the occasion of particular festivals, such as Corpus Christi, Christmas and New Year.

4. The situation of Quito seems to be different, although we did not carry out a detailed study of the city. Roast guinea-pig is mainly served in cafés close to the markets and in food stalls in working-class neighbourhoods. Traditional-cuisine restaurants for the middle classes and for tourists do not have guinea-pig on their menu: guinea-pig in Quito is a 'popular' and mestizo dish. I have noticed that, in order to make guinea-pig more acceptable on the 'set' menu served at a tavern near the Carolina Plaza, there was guinea-pig cooked in breadcrumbs, a kind of 'Wiener schnitzel' guinea-pig – an innovative urban variation that did not exist in any of the places we visited during our fieldwork. It is highly likely that, while I am writing (1991), the guinea-pig will have reached menus in many of the places I have discussed

in this chapter. This would mean the 'symbolic death' of the guinea-pig, its bodily disappearance and its transformation into a squashed and harmless piece of meat. The fact of eating it will no longer be a cause for anxiety – much the same process that frog undergoes when it is transformed into 'frog's legs' or veal into 'Wiener schnitzel'.

5. There are, then, two customary forms of consumption: what we might call 'familial', where at least two members of the family decide to eat guinea-pig, and the mainly 'masculine', when a group of friends, all men, decide to have a party or simply to organize an outing to eat roast guinea-pig and drink aguardiente in a popular tavern. Due to the price of guinea-pig, we can expect the second type of consumption to predominate in the Ecuadorean sierra – an 'anthropological intuition' which needs to be verified by more data.

CHAPTER SEVEN

Social and Cultural Logics

In Chapter 2 I discussed the concept of cultural and social complexity. The first refers to the quantity of information produced
and circulated in a particular setting, in other words the knowledge
that actors use to face the world. The concept of social complexity,
on the other hand, refers to kinds of social interaction. I believe it
is important to maintain this analytical distinction, even if it may
appear arbitrary, since in the empirical reality the social cannot
be separated from the cultural and vice versa. The social life
the anthropologist studies is a set of activities on the part of
specific actors in a physical and social environment. Obviously
these activities are charged with intentionality; they are based
upon a 'capital' of knowledge and therefore initiate a process
of interpretation that involves the majority of participants. This
definition would be adequate for defining the object of study and
methodology if we were only dealing with hypotheses of social
change. However, social action does not always reproduce what is
existing. It can also create the new and try to change the world.
These ideas imply that social actors enter into mutual relationships
based on consensus and agreement, but not necessarily all the time.
The problem, then, is how to conceptualize discontinuities, discrepancies and, at the extreme, conflicts, which generate novel,
'effervescent' conditions that stimulate the questioning of both the
models of interpretation of realities which are legitimized and the
social statuses involved. The distinction between social and cultural
spheres acquires meaning through this conceptualization.

Geertz (1959), in an article written before he developed a mainly
culturalist focus and in which his objective was the explanation of
social change, rightly questioned the distinction between the social
and the cultural spheres. He argues that even if in practice these
spheres are mutually interdependent, they still have to be treated

as if they were independent. The problem of the integration of the cultural and social spheres is, in the end, an empirical issue. The cultural sphere is the field of beliefs, of expressive symbols and of values which actors employ to define the world, to express their feelings and to formulate normative judgements. The social sphere embraces the concrete forms of social interaction and the way the web of social relations is constituted. Although we may find a situation of isomorphism as between the social and the cultural spheres, generally speaking, in most societies there are discontinuities between the two. In other words, the majority of what is believed to exist is what is actually done – but not all of it. Geertz's hypothesis about change derives from this lack of correspondence between these two systems, since what is believed cannot be acted out completely and unequivocally. In the changing context of Java, Geertz finds incongruity as between the content of religious beliefs and the rules of social interaction. Ritual developed in a rural context of specific social relations is not effective in an urban context. In a rural context kinship relations and proximity reinforce and make possible the development of rituals, while in the urban context relationships of class, work or political goals predominate (1959, p. 1011).[1]

One of the main problems with this type of theoretical model, despite its advantages over the strictly functionalist model, is that people still believe that the cultural sphere is 'integrated logically' and that there is a conceptual and stylistic unity, based on fundamental agreements about systems of meaning and dominant values. In the social sphere, likewise, the model postulates that there is a sort of functional integration between social positions and the fulfilment of roles. Therefore discontinuities exist only between, and not within, the social and the cultural spheres. So neither the social nor the cultural spheres are perfectly integrated: in every society there will be conceptual and normative differences as well as discrepancies in social integration. We do not wish to overstate this hypothesis, though – this would be to go to the opposite extreme to functionalism: to argue that everything changes all the time and that, consequently, society lives in a state of more or less permanent anarchy. Experience shows that, in fact, such conditions only occur at particular moments in the history of societies.

It is therefore more realistic to think of societies studied by anthropologists, especially today, as having different models of reality interpretation as well as different fields of social interaction.

One of the great problems that exists in any culture, at any time, is how to organize diversity rather then simply to produce uniformity. In order to avoid the post-modernist trap, we need to try to understand and resolve the problem of how social and cultural production and reproduction take place.[2] In my view, this calls for the introduction of elements of power, linking it with mechanisms that legitimize belief and with the models for interpreting reality used by actors in social life. Our sample study, hopefully, may contribute to a better understanding of these processes.

Power and Legitimization

I do not intend to develop this matter in great detail or to summarize the achievements and drawbacks of different theories. Other people have done this already, and better.[3] Rather, I shall follow the line of enquiry developed by Wolf (1990), which will allow me to extend his analysis to the concrete development project that was the starting-point of our analysis. Wolf distinguishes four types of power. The first is a characteristic mainly of the individual, an attribute of the person (such as to speak of a 'charismatic' man or woman). The second refers to the capacity of a concrete ego to condition an alter so that he/she follows the ego's will. The third, even if still at an interactional level, places special emphasis on ways a person exercises control or influence over a group of people or over a social unit, inducing it to act in a certain way in a specific social context – what Wolf calls 'tactical power or organizational power' (1990, p. 586). Lastly, the fourth not only influences social contexts, but also creates them, thus structuring other people's field of action. This type of power refers not only to 'awareness control' or the 'shaping or conditioning of mentalities and way of thinking', but also to control over resources that actors need in order to assure their material reproduction as capital or as a labour force – what Wolf calls 'structural' power.

From the standpoint of a 'realistic' anthropology – concerned with conditions of reproduction, with social and cultural change – the last two types of power are the most relevant. The original objective of the programme of developing the production of guinea-pigs was to change 'existing methods of production by introducing new techniques and information'. The Ministry of Agriculture and Animal Husbandry therefore became an agent of power, via the activities of bureaucrats, experts and rural development workers, who controlled the allocation of primary material resources in order to promote economic and social development. A project of this kinds aims above all at 'changing the mentality of people' and 'introducing new ideas which lead to changes in conditions of production', rather than at controlling the material conditions of reproduction. Material resources – improved guinea-pigs and facilities – are no more than an 'instrumental' tool used to achieve the central goal of a 'modernizing of mentalities'. The legitimation of different models and productive practices are obviously involved.

It is important to point out that the actors involved are on the one hand, women and, on the other, rural development workers. In no case are scientific 'experts', whatever the capital knowledge they possess, those who ensure the application of one productive model rather than another. In the case of producing guinea-pigs, knowledge is accumulated and transmitted through a kind of practice which is part of a broader knowledge of plants and animals. Rural development workers pass on the 'findings' of experts – scientists and veterinarians – who, in ideal experimental conditions, establish adequate dietary rules and the right kind of health care. In other words, rural development workers constitute the last step in a technological model of transformation based on 'scientific knowledge'.

In any interaction, power lies in the capacity of certain actors to impose one of the models available as the 'only one', because it is the most effective, valid or sacred or because it seems more convincing. If this is successful, other models disappear and will be replaced by successful interpretations and practices (Wolf, 1990, p. 593). Consequently consensus – the ultimate goal of power – results in an impoverishment of reality in the sense that alternative knowledge and practices tend to disappear or, in the face of the supremacy of one form of knowledge, survive only as resistance or become secondary forms of social interaction, limited and marginalized. This 'diversity of models and practices' is visible at many levels in Ecuadorean society.[4]

The empirical findings discussed here have shown the existence of important cultural and social differences, which can be explained, firstly, by discontinuities as between general, peasant, popular understanding on the one hand and scientific knowledge on the other, and, secondly, by differences in modes of social and cultural circulation of guinea-pigs, due to uncertain variations in ethnic boundaries on a small scale. The case of the guinea-pig shows these discontinuities on a small scale.

Without wishing to complicate the analysis already presented, it is important, none the less, to add the problematic of legitimization of models and social practices to the element of power. The analysis of the ways in which different discourses and interpretations of reality are presented is as important as the examination of their content. The more flexible the form used, the higher the potential as legitimation. The peasant model is an 'oral' understanding, transmitted from mother to daughter through active participation in rituals where guinea-pig meat is circulated. The cooking of guinea-pigs cannot exist without this type of female labour, just as the hygiene and the health of guinea-pigs cannot be ensured without the transmission of beliefs about the hot and the cold. There is no book which can be consulted; there are no precise historical references, with detailed case-studies, which show alternative norms to follow in fields such as hygiene or the feeding and health care of animals. Nor are there any veterinary experts, as there are *curanderos* and *sobadores*, who can help to cure animals. The oral culture of the guinea-pig is, therefore, a local and democratic knowledge.

On the contrary, 'scientific knowledge' of the guinea-pig is based on accumulated experience and derives from academic thinking. The development of chemistry, biology and medical science in general, together with the practice of these kinds of knowledge, distinguishes the 'world of animals' from the 'world of plants' and both of them from 'the world of humans'. Well-known specialist treatises on the 'exact' sciences (at least for social scientists) are treated as valid not only as they were originally written, but also because it is always possible – when necessary – to come back and look at them again critically. Scientific knowledge, then, lies outside peasant 'local knowledge': the truths it embodies are here and now, and the here and now embraces the whole universe. One important consequence of this logic is that accumulated knowledge tends to become detached from moral issues and from social and political obligations (Gellner, 1974, p. 166). In its extreme forms, this can generate a type of division – the idea that all that can be done should actually be done, and that, in principle, every modification and technological change is an improvement. To deny it is to invite being accused of conservatism and traditionalism. Such an ideology would not be possible without the existence of claims for universality. Findings about guinea-pigs are seen as being equally valid in Palmira Dávalos as in Quito, in Quito as in Lusaka, in Ecuador as in Burkino Faso. It is a claim, though, that would never be accepted by an Ecuadorean peasant.

Moreover, this position can be seen in a broader way in both the technical records of rural development workers, who are not experts in the breeding of guinea-pigs, and in manuals given out to producers. The power of this approach is claimed to lie not just in its presumed efficacy in increasing production and productivity, but also in the flexible adaptation of specialist knowledge to the pragmatic needs of a public with different 'logics' and 'interests'.

On the one hand, then, we have the peasant style of thought, a 'popular' style that can also be found in the urban world. This kind of reasoning is based on a set of beliefs which appear not merely as abstractions, but which acquire their full meaning when they are acted out in the world, when they are turned into normative and social practices. 'Interests' and 'preferences' acquire, from the outset, a central social character. The oral culture of the guinea-pig, with all its social and symbolic complexity, is a good example, which stands in juxtaposition to the scientific knowledge of modernizers, who require total dissociation of empirical fact from values. For them, truth is established (or has to be obtained) independently of possible value judgements. In this logic, it is not important that guinea-pigs circulate in 'traditional' ways in feasts and in healing ceremonies, since forms of 'cultural consumption' cannot, in principle, influence or determine productive strategies. It is obvious that this is a model in which the 'rationality' of the actors is not the only main axiom, but where people choose what they prefer because it is more 'useful'. Preferences and interests that affect choice are articulated simply as 'private' (Hefner, 1983, p. 669).

It is obvious that an anthropological model, on the other hand, based on a very detailed description of beliefs and social practices, insists on the strict relationship that exists between 'choice' and normative or social preferences. Likewise, preferences are seen not only as the maximization of individual wishes but as manifestations of institutional and structural power. At this point, even extreme rationalists and modernizers would have to accept that, in the end, their kinds of 'cognitive activity' are real and, in a very tangible way, 'extraterritorial', non-local. Accepting this leaves out the vital experience of everyday life, based on important social ties and the importance of normative choices. 'Scientific' thinking, on the other hand, assumes the universality ('extraterritoriality') of these kinds of considerations, which cannot be omitted if one is to ensure the progress of 'objective' knowledge. The model of 'traditional' rural development which stems from this logic can only work if we accept the existence of an abstract 'rational' producer. When reality shows that the predicted changes are not taking place at the expected pace, doubts about the efficacy of the model appear to be filtered out by the social practice that is experienced.

The Implementation of Social and Cultural Change: Outcomes, Dilemmas and Paradoxes

New sets of technological measures, then, entail the introduction of more variables in the productive process, new and varied productive components and therefore a more focused task for the producer in the care and control of specific elements. The philosophy of the development project is based on what we might call the 'existence of hypothetical needs of the population', the basic postulate being that the women's need for 'more and better guinea-pigs' was not fulfilled. Throughout this book, on the other hand, I have tried to show that traditional ways of breeding and producing guinea-pigs, which take place at individual and social levels, are 'preferential needs' that are closely related to the way in which animals circulate in symbolic and social arenas. If we are right in our ethnographic analysis, we have to acknowledge that both the general social environment and the local institutional power influence effective preferences and consequently choices. The creation of new 'needs' – the object of any project of technological and productive change – implies that the population has to change preferences which are closely linked to wider social and cultural processes.

The guinea-pig project was only implemented in four communities: Tigualó, Chirinche and Llactahurco in the area of the programme of Integrated Rural Development in Salcedo, and in Guzo, which is part of the programme of Quimiag-Penipe. But the ambitious aim of incorporating the majority of mothers and housewives in the modernization programme for rearing guinea-pigs has not, in fact, been achieved anywhere. In all these communities, a small minority has agreed to participate in the programme: at the individual level, we found eight women in Llactahurco, the same number in Tigualó and five in Guzo, while in Chirinche there was a 'communal, cooperative' project in which a few women decided to take part. To understand these processes the problem is where to put the emphasis: on the minority of women that do take part or on the women who refuse to participate. The reasons for following either option will vary accordingly to particular situations and responses to the rural development workers and to the Integrated Rural Development programme which reveal the cultural plurality referred to at the beginning of the chapter. It therefore becomes necessary to understand the logic of those women who did agree to become 'modern' producers of guinea-pigs.

A preliminary answer can be found in the 'condition of being a woman'. It is obvious that the programme constitutes 'one more worry', 'another thing to pay attention to' on top of the multiple domestic and productive activities that require the presence of a 'housewife'. Generally speaking, housework and productive work vary over time and are related to the domestic family cycle. In a situation where the ratio between consumers and producers is unfavourable, female work will be more intensive if she has smaller children. The situation changes, though, when her daughters begin to help her with the housework. In terms of an 'ideal' demographic cycle, after fifteen years of marriage things will change, coinciding with the end of the average fertility span. In other words, when a woman approaches the age of forty, she receives more help and can therefore feel freer to engage in new activities – the most common life condition among those producers who participated in the pilot experiment, many being older than fifty.

Age coincides with a parallel change in the perception of a woman that she will become 'mature', 'experienced', 'more knowledgeable' and more 'independent'. Masculine control also tends to decrease, and a woman gains more freedom of movement.[5] The transaction from 'mother' to 'grandmother' is therefore central. Women acquire an authority that derives from years of experience and because their advice is sought by their newly married children. In the reproduction of the family, women are the repositories of kinds of knowledge which are greatly appreciated, especially in relation to health care and sickness.

These dynamics have to be taken into account if we want to

understand those processes of change. Young women, on the other hand, need to behave themselves and are basically defined as 'immature', 'dependent' and 'lacking in authority'. But this changes with age, and women can become, at least in principle and paradoxically, 'more open' to new stimuli. None the less, from their perspective, it is important to maintain a balance between 'independence' and 'wisdom'. With age, women accumulate a 'capital of knowledge' which gives them both authority and the opportunity to take up important roles in the local transmission of cultural practices. This includes knowledge capital related to guinea-pig production.

We should remember, though, that we are in a changing field, where producers of these animals, which have 'traditional', symbolic and social significance, may be totally absent from the new 'products' that the development project is trying to introduce. The guinea-pig is an old 'product', rooted in a set of beliefs and creeds that are very strong and embodied in oral tradition. Changing 'local traditions' radically carries with it certain risks, among them the 'loss of prestige' – whose importance should not been underestimated. On the one hand, the preservation of social status and the centrality of networking are cardinal in women's strategies. On the other hand, cultural change more generally leads actors to perceive their beliefs or doctrines as inconsistent with or as inadequate guarantees of social reproduction.[6] It is important to point out that women 'transform' the technological changes that have been introduced by attempting to solve these social and cultural dilemmas. In nearly all cases in which individuals have adapted to new technologies, there has been adjustment as between the project of the technical experts and the rural development workers and local knowledge and practice: the result is a 'third' model or various 'third' models of breeding which are neither 'traditional' nor 'modern'. In Tigualó, for instance, the most significant changes are the use of new facilities and the incorporation of 'improved' male guinea-pigs, which people nevertheless keep in traditional hutches made with leftovers of alfalfa, weeds and ashes. Likewise, certain healing practices, which have been discussed previously, are still alive and there is no sign of change.

In Llactahurco, the only changes that had been embraced were the same as those in Tigualó: new services and new male breeding-stock. However, we observed that traditional practices are still employed and there is a 'lack of confidence' in modern practices.

Here are a few examples. People installed 'fireplaces' at the side of the new hutches to maintain warmth and to prevent cold from making the guinea-pigs sick or killing them. They also filled crates with barley straw and medical herbs, and, in order to defend the hutches from attacks by other animals, they sprinkled chillies, powder and ashes around as well as cleaning the outside with water of boiled fish. Likewise, traditional practices were still carried out to control mating: pregnant mothers and newborn guinea-pigs were not separated from the rest of the animals. This implies that, in practice, there is only one hutch, with no separation by sex, age or general condition. None the less, in some cases, there were two living-spaces: in one, there were Peruvian guinea-pigs – the 'improved' male – and in the other the rest of the animals.

Undoubtedly the most important finding is that people keep the hutch in the kitchen, even when they join modern, technological projects. This implies, then, not only that they distrust the efficacy of the programme, but also that the 'new' guinea-pigs are raised for the market, while the *runas* are for internal consumption. Another additional point was that the 'new' animals can be sold at a higher price since they 'have more value'. In Tigualó, on the other hand, we found that many female producers, who had similar attitudes, had decided to eat the improved guinea-pigs too. Some of them found this type of guinea-pig 'tasty', with 'very sweet' meat.

By Way of Conclusion: Change and Development

This book should be seen as an encounter between different social and cultural logics. These differences coexist in a common territorial space, express different 'historicities' and are part of the political arena, in both developed and developing countries, where the logic of the modern state is based on the implementation of a more or less permanent programme of economic development. Our ethnography and the study of particular cases show discontinuities and contradictions between these logics, but they can help our understanding of social and cultural change. 'Marginal' cases of change indicate that – as we showed in the first few pages of this chapter – transformation is possible since it takes place within a context of power relations. Women who reject the new technological programme, cannot, in principle, be penalized, because the power of the experts and of rural development workers is limited. On the other hand, we should not forget that, even if the programmes are based on a logic of hypothetical needs, the orthodox philosophy of these projects is reformist, that is to say, it is expected that the actors themselves will define their goals in the end. Obviously, people always hope that these aims will coincide with the objectives of the project, since these are thought of as being most 'valid and appropriate' for solving the problems which gave rise to the process of intervention. None the less, even if the women who embrace it adopt part of the methodological proposals, in practice they show independence and originality, and develop different solutions based on conserving 'knowledge capital' which has been accumulated for a long time. This 'capital' allows them to preserve acquired social status. So these women show double independence and originality: firstly when they accept the technological programme, and secondly when they reaffirm the validity of knowledge acquired in the past about health and animals.

Our first lesson can be formulated as follow: the existence of power relations necessarily requires the anthropologist to examine the degree of autonomy that actors have. Therefore, the central issue becomes the understanding of how social actors express their autonomy and maintain it over time. Conceptions of institutional and structural power are therefore of primary importance. This generalization, however, even though it acknowledges objective 'inequalities' in the means and resources that social actors can draw upon, does not enable us to forecast the result that will occur. In principle, the result appears open, even if the range of possibilities and solutions is not limitless.[7]

The second lesson is that 'culture' is an essential component of the way in which the guinea-pig is produced, consumed and circulated. These ideas, too, are part of a productive scheme; they are not separated from material needs. 'Peasants' and 'experts' have different reference systems, which are connected to different economic models. If we accept this perspective, we are obviously in a position to think of change as a part of production in general. People do change their ideas and beliefs in order to solve technical problems, so that innovations are tried out or accepted. This is true both for the peasant and for the expert who engages in self-criticism.

The third lesson relates to the complexity of preference schedules of needs and their formation. I have tried to demonstrate how symbolic knowledge and productive practices are combined in the daily lives of these women in the context of changes in biological and social time, as women shift from being 'dependent' to becoming 'more independent'. These processes open up new social spaces and generate other kinds of discontinuity, which constitute new cultural elements. Actors can find new positions and establish alliances that increase their social as well as their economic possibilities. Undoubtedly, an increase in the number of guinea-pigs available increases the possibility of selling a surplus, at the same time increasing the intake of protein. Nevertheless, this type of change can result in increased inequality in participation in rituals and ceremonies, since it is possible to 'make a contribution' and 'to offer' more and better guinea-pigs. On the other hand, as we have seen, improved guinea-pigs enter the system of domestic and ritual consumption. Whatever the answer is, the resulting social and cultural complexity is remote from the kind of 'subjective model' that assumes automatic adjustment between prices, or quantity of protein, and producers' preferences. The careful examination of the social and moral contexts that lie behind definitions of needs, preference schedules, and consumption is a satisfactory approximation, although, with all its virtues and pitfalls, this book illustrates the importance of trying to understand the guinea-pig in all its social and symbolic complexity. However, even after this has been done, to the great disappointment of 'modernizers', we cannot convert our findings into recipes that can be easily put into practice. Unfortunately, since 'people want to change themselves', they feel and act in their own ways. The results, then, can never be mathematically predicted.

Notes

1. Later, Geertz stressed the autonomy of culture in relation to social structure and to individual psychology. In the last analysis, his model of 'thick description' develops from an assumption about the inner coherence of culture, which is consequently possible only in historically stable periods. It is important to point out, though, that in the article I have already mentioned (1959) Geertz explicitly refers

to the motivational structure of the individual as a third level in the process of tracing out discontinuities that help us to understand social change. To a certain extent, Geertz also implies that culture is integrated via some overriding logical principle, while change is to be explained via discontinuities as between culture and society.

2. As a consequence of 'post-modernist' debate in anthropology, the traditional use of concepts such as culture and society has been questioned by anthropologists who have absolutely refused to be associated with the earlier post-modernists (Keesing, 1987; Strathern, 1987). One of the most systematic criticisms of post-modernism and deconstructionism has been developed by Bailey (1991).

3. In my opinion the small book by Lukes (1974), although written some time ago, is still a 'classic' on the problematic of power. Gellner (1973) is useful for an understanding of the legitimacy of beliefs.

4. Gellner has shown that the existence of a plurality of options open to individuals – together with an idea of choice – is a necessary but not sufficient condition for the development of modernity (1974, p. 156). The central point, he infers, is to shift from individual choice to the analysis of 'styles of thinking'. At this level, the appearance of the 'style' which we might characterize as 'scientific' is undoubtedly an essential component. Obviously this shift of emphasis – from the concrete individual who has doubts about the multiplicity of options to something as abstract as a 'style of thinking' – gives rise to a set of difficulties, which we cannot explore here in detail.

5. Stølen (1988) has convincingly analysed changes in women's condition and kinship relations in accordance with age, among a peasant mestizo population. Here I assume, in a rather arbitrary way, that the same may be true in Indian communities.

6. Gellner has warned about the difficulties that anthropologists have to face when they practise a policy of indulgence toward their informants without being conceptually coherent, by making it possible for them to manipulate each other:

> Excessive indulgence in contextual charity blinds us to what is worst in the life of societies. It blinds us to the possibility that social change may occur through the replacement of an inconsistent doctrine or ethic by a better one, or through a more consistent application of either. It equally blinds us to the possibility of, for instance, social control through the employment of absurd, ambiguous, inconsistent or unintelligible doctrines. (1970, pp. 42–3)

7. One promising focus of enquiry has been developed by Long (1989, 1990). Following this line of thought, our case-study could be conceptualized as a typical situation of contact between individuals and

units which represent different interests and are backed up by different resources. Long insists on the need to consider, for obvious methodological reasons, case-studies where there has been 'planned' intervention by the state (1989, pp. 3–6).

Bibliography

Acero Coral, G. and Pianalto de Dalle Rive, M.A. (1985) *Medicina indígena. Cacha-Chimborazo*. Quito: Ediciones Abya-Ayala.

Aguiló, F. (1987) *El hombre del Chimborazo*. Quito: Ediciones Abya-Ayala.

Aguirre Palma, B. (1987) *Religiosidad del campesino de Otón*. Quito: Ediciones Abya-Ayala.

Anderson, E.N. (1980) '"Heating" and "cooling" foods in Hong Kong and Taiwan'. *Social Science Information* 19 (2): 237-68.

Anon. (1978) *Biblioteca Agropecuaria. Cuy: Alimento popular*. Lima: Editorial Mercurio.

Appadurai, A. (1988) 'How to make a national cuisine: Cookbooks in contemporary India'. *Comparative Studies in Society and History* 30 (1): 3-24.

Archetti, E.P. (1986) 'Et antropologisk perspektiv på kulturell endring og utvikling'. *Internasjonal Politikk* 4-5: 35-60.

Bailey, F.G. (1991) *The Prevalence of Deceit*. Ithaca: Cornell University Press.

Balladelli, P.P. (1988) *Entre lo mágico y lo natural: La medicina indígena. Testimonios de Pesillo*. Quito: Ediciones Abya-Ayala.

Barahona, C. (1982) 'La Soba de cuy'. In J. Sánches Parga, C. Barahona, G. Ramón, R. Harari, O. Flores and A. P. Castelnouvo, *Política de salud y comunidad andina*. Quito: CAAP Editores.

Barthes, R. (1979) 'Toward a psychology of contemporary food consumption'. In R. Foster and O. Ranum (eds), *Food and Drink in History*. Baltimore: Johns Hopkins University Press.

Bianchi, A. (1986) *Hierbas medicinales de Cotopaxi*. Quito: Ediciones Abya-Ayala.

Bolton, R. (1979) 'Guinea pig, protein, and ritual'. *Ethnology* 18: 229-52.

Bolton, R. and Calvin, L. (1981) 'El cuy en la cultura peruana contemporánea'. In H. Lechman and A.M. Soldi (eds), *La tecnología en el mundo andino*. Mexico City: Universidad Nacional Autónoma de México.

Borneman, J. (1988) 'Race, ethnicity, species, breed: totemism and horse-breed classification in America'. *Comparative Studies in Society and History* 30 (1): 25-51.

Bougerol, C. (1985) 'Logique de l'excès, logique de la rupture: le chaud et le froid dans la médicine populaire guadeloupéenne'. *L'Ethnographie* 96–97 (2–3): 159–68.

Bourdieu, P. (1980) *Le sens pratique*. Paris: Minuit.

Bromley, R.J. (1975) 'Periodic and daily markets in Highland Ecuador'. Doctoral thesis, Cambridge University.

—— (1976) 'Contemporary market periodicity in Highland Ecuador'. In C.A. Smith (ed.), *Regional Analysis*. London/New York: Academic Press.

—— (1978) 'Traditional and modern change in the growth of systems of market centres in Highland Ecuador'. In R.H.T. Smith (ed.), *Marketplace Trade: Periodic Markets, Hawkers and Traders in Africa, Asia and Latin America*. Vancouver: University of British Columbia Press.

Castaño Quintero, M. (1981) *Explotación del curi o cuy*. Bogotá: Ministerio de Agricultura.

Chivilchez Chávez, J. (1980) *Enfermedades y política sanitaria en la crianza de cuyes*. Huancayo: Universidad Nacional del Centro del Perú.

Currier, R. (1966) 'The hot–cold syndrome and symbolic balance in Mexican and Spanish-American folk medicine'. *Ethnology* 5: 251–63.

Digard, J.P. (1990) *L'Homme et les animaux domestiques*. Paris: Fayard.

Doña Juanita (1986) *Cocina tradicional del Ecuador*. Quito: Gangotena y Ruiz Editores.

Douglas, M. (1975) *Implicit Meanings*. London: Routledge & Kegan Paul.

Douglas, M. and Gross, J. (1981) 'Food and culture: Measuring the intricacy of rule systems'. *Social Science Information* 20 (1): 1–35.

Escobar, G. and Escobar, G. (1972) 'Observaciones etnográficas sobre la crianza y los usos del cuye en la región de Cuzco'. *Antropología Andina* 1–2: 34–49.

Estrella, E. (1978) *Medicina aborigen. La práctica médica aborigen de la Sierra ecuatoriana*. Quito: Editorial Epoca.

Fischler, C. (1980) 'Food habits, social change and the nature/culture dilemma'. *Social Science Information* 19 (6): 937–53.

Foster, G. (1953) 'Relationships between Spanish and Spanish-American folk medicine'. *Journal of American Folklore* 6: 201–17.

—— (1978) 'Disease etiologies in non-western medical systems'. *American Anthropologist* 78 (4): 773–82.

—— (1979) 'Methodological problems in the study of intracultural variation: The hot/cold dichotomy in Tzintzuntzan'. *Human Organization* 38 (3): 179–83.

Freire, M. (1988) 'El cuy en la cultura indígena: algunos aspectos de su importancia'. *Hombre y ambiente* 1 (5): 117–29.

Fried, M.O. (1986) *Comidas del Ecuador. Recetas tradicionales para gente de hoy*. Quito: published by author.

Friedberg, C. (1985) 'La santé à Bali: le plein, le temperé et le juste milieu'. *L'Ethnographie* 96–97 (2–3): 141–58.

Fuentealba, G. (1985) 'La comida como práctica simbólica y ritual (Una aproximación a la cultura indígena y proceso de cambio)'. *Ecuador Debate* 9: 183–98.

Gade, D.W. (1957) 'The Guinea pig in Andean folk culture'. *The Geographical Review* 57 (2): 213–24.

Geertz, C. (1959) 'Ritual and social change: A Javanese example'. *American Anthropologist* 61: 991–1012.

Gellner, E. (1970) 'Concepts and society'. In B.R. Wilson (ed.), *Rationality*. London: Basil Blackwell.

Gellner, E. (1974) *The Legitimation of Belief*. Cambridge: Cambridge University Press.

Goody, J. (1982) *Cooking, Cuisine and Class: A Study in Comparative Sociology*. Cambridge: Cambridge University Press.

Hanssen-Bauer, J. (1982) *Plaza Pachano. Market Integration, Intermediaries and Rural Differentiation in Tungurahua, Ecuador*. Oslo Occasional Papers in Social Anthropology, 5. Oslo: Department of Social Anthropology, University of Oslo.

Hefner, R.W. (1983) 'The problem of preference: Economic and ritual change in Highlands Java'. *Man* 18 (4): 669–89.

Heras, L., Barreto, N., Marquez, J., Marquez, M., Cabrera, I., Aucay, L., Aucay C. and Guamán L. (1985) 'Consumo alimenticio, conocimiento y prácticas: El caso Pucará y Shagly'. *Ecuador Debate* 9: 201–19.

Ingold, T. (ed.) (1988) *What is an Animal?* London: Allen & Unwin.

Jordan, N. de (1979) *Nuestras comidas*. Cochabamba: published by author.

Keesing, R. (1987) 'Anthropology as interpretative quest'. *Current Anthropology* 28: 161–76.

King, J. (1956) 'Social relations of the domestic guinea pig living under semi-natural conditions'. *Ecology* 37: 221–8.

Lange, F. (1975) *Manger ou les jeux et les creux du plat*. Paris: Editions du Seuil.

Leach, E. (1970) *Lévi-Strauss*. London: Fontana/Collins.

Lehrer, A. (1969) 'Semantic cuisine'. *Journal of Linguistics* 5 (1): 39–56.

—— (1972) 'Cooking vocabularies and the culinary triangle of Lévi-Strauss'. *Anthropological Linguistics* 14 (1): 155–71.

LERT (1982) *Sabrosos platos criollos*. Quito: Libreria Selecciones.

Lévi-Strauss, C. (1965) 'Le triangle culinaire'. *L'Arc* 26: 19–29.

—— (1968) *L'Origine des manières de table*. Paris: Plon.

Logan, M. (1972) 'Humoral folk medicine: A potential aid in controlling Pellagra in Mexico'. *Ethnomedicine* 1 (3–4): 397–410.

—— (1973) 'Humoral medicine in Guatemala and peasant acceptance of modern medicine'. *Human Organization* 32 (4): 385–95.

Long, N. (ed.) (1989) *Encounters at the Interface. A Perspective on Social Discontinuities in Rural Development*. Wageningen: Agricultural University.

—— (1990) ' From paradigm lost to paradigm regained? The case for an actor-oriented sociology of development'. *European Review of Latin American and Caribbean Studies* 49: 3–24.

Lukes, S. (1974) *Power: A Radical View*. London: Macmillan.

—— (1977) *Essays in Social Theory*. London: Macmillan.

Luna de la Fuente, C. and Moreno Rojas, A.E. (1969) *El cuy. Recomendaciones para su crianza*. Lima: Universidad Agraria de La Molina.

McKee, L. (1988) 'Tratamiento etnomédico de las enfermedades diarreicas de los niños en la Sierra del Ecuador'. In L. McKee and S. Argüello (eds), *Nuevas investigaciones antropológicas ecuatorianas*. Quito: Ediciones Abya-Ayala.

Mintz, S. (1985) *Sweetness and Power. The Place of Sugar in Modern History*. New York: Viking Penguin Books.

Moya, R. (1981) *Simbolismo y ritual en el Ecuador andino*. Colección Pendoneros, 40. Otavalo: Instituto Otavaleño de Antropologia.

Muñoz Bernand, C. (1986) *Enfermedad, daño e ideología. Antropología médica de los Renacientes de Pindilig*. Quito: Ediciones Abya-Ayala.

Muratorio, B. (1982) *Etnicidad, evangelización y protesta en el Ecuador*. Quito: Ediciones CIESE.

Naranjo, M. (coord.) (1986) *Cultura popular en el Ecuador. Cotopaxi*. Quito: Centro Interamericano de artesanias y artes populares.

Nicod, M. (1975) 'A method of eliciting the social meaning of food'. MS thesis, University of London.

Ordóñez de Cobos, C. (1984) *Cocina moderna*. Cuenca: published by author.

Parry, J. and Bloch, M. (eds) (1989) *Money and the Morality of Exchange*. Cambridge: Cambridge University Press.

Polo de Ondegardo, J. (1916) *Los errores y supersticiones de los indios, sacados del tratado y averiguación que hizo el licenciado Polo*. In Colección de libros y documentos referentes a la historia del Perú, edited by H.H. Urteaga, ser.1, Tomo III, pp. 45–188. Imprenta y Librería Sarandí: Lima.

Poma de Ayala, G. (1956) *La nueva crónica y buen gobierno*. Editorial Cultura, Dirección de Cultura, Arquelogía e Historia del Ministerio de Educación Pública del Perú: Lima.

Rueda, M.V. (1982) *La fiesta religiosa campesina (Andes ecuatorianos)*. Quito: Ediciones de la Universidad Católica.

Sahlins, M. (1976) *Culture and Practical Reason*. Chicago: University of Chicago Press.

Sallnow, M.J. (1991) 'Pilgrimage and cultural fracture in the Andes'. In J. Eade and M.J.Sallnow (eds), *Contesting the Sacred. The Anthropology of Christian Pilgrimage*. London: Routledge.

Sánchez Parga, J. (1985) 'Condiciones y comportamientos alimenticios en una zona serrana: Sigchos'. *Ecuador Debate* 9: 257–78.

Sánchez Parga, J., Barahona, C., Ramón, G., Harari, R., Flores, O. and

Castelnouvo, A.P. (1982) *Política de salud y comunidad andina*. Quito: CAAP editores.

Serpell, J. (1986) *In the Company of Animals*. Oxford: Basil Blackwell.

Sousa, L. and Chalampuente, L. (1980) *Manual para la crianza de cuyes a nivel casero*. Quito: Proyecto PNUD-FAO ECU/78/004.

Stølen, K.A. (1988) 'Control y dominación en las relaciones de género: un estudio de caso en la Sierra ecuatoriana'. *Iberoamericana. Nordic Journal of Latin American Studies* 18 (2): 3–32.

Strathern, M. (1987) 'Out of context: The persuasive fictions of anthropology'. *Current Anthropology* 28: 251–81.

Tambiah, S.J. (1981) ' A performative approach to ritual'. *The Proceedings of the British Academy* vol. LXV: 113–69.

Tannahill, R. (1973) *Food in History*. London: Methuen.

Turner, V. (1974) *Dramas, Fields and Metaphors*. Ithaca, New York: Cornell University Press.

Vialles, N. (1987) *Le Sang et la chair. Les abattoirs des pays de l'Adour*. Paris: Editions de la Maison des Sciences de L'homme.

White, A. (1982) *Hierbas del Ecuador*. Quito: Libri Mundi.

Wing, E.S. (1975) 'La domesticación de animales en los Andes'. *Allpanchis* 8 (1): 25–44.

Wolf, E. (1990) 'Facing power – Old insights, new questions'. *American Anthropologist* 92 (3): 586–96.

Zevallos, D. (1980) *El cuy. Su crianza y explotación*. Lima: San Martín.

Index